COMING TO LONDON

COMING TO
LONDON

by William Plomer, Leonard Woolf, V. S.
Pritchett, George Barker, J. B. Priestley
Elizabeth Bowen, Geoffrey Grigson
John Middleton Murry, Christopher
Isherwood, Alan Pryce-Jones
William Sansom, Jocelyn
Brooke, Rose Macaulay
and Edith Sitwell

Edited by
JOHN LEHMANN

Essay Index Reprint Series

 BOOKS FOR LIBRARIES PRESS
FREEPORT, NEW YORK

INTERNATIONAL STANDARD BOOK NUMBER:
0-8369-2409-6

LIBRARY OF CONGRESS CATALOG CARD NUMBER:
73-152189

PRINTED IN THE UNITED STATES OF AMERICA
BY
NEW WORLD BOOK MANUFACTURING CO., INC.
HALLANDALE, FLORIDA 33009

CONTENTS

THE idea of preparing a series of reminiscences under
the general title of 'Coming to London' originated, to
the best of my recollection, at an editorial luncheon of
The London Magazine held at my house. I was in the
habit, in those early days, of inviting the members of
our editorial board to meet over luncheon every two or
three months, to review the progress of the magazine
and to discuss future plans. My hope always was that
some new idea, fertile in opportunities of exploitation,
would be born, almost spontaneously, in the unforced
to-and-fro of discussion and argument. And so it was on
this occasion. Miss Elizabeth Bowen, Mr John Hay-
ward, Mr William Plomer, Mr Rex Warner and Dr
C. V. Wedgwood were, I remember, present; in fact
the whole editorial board as then constituted. We
were all agreed in believing that one of the most
useful services that *The London Magazine* could perform—as well as one of the most pleasant for its readers—was to encourage distinguished writers to put
down their reminiscences of the literary past on paper;
reminiscences that might otherwise never have been
recorded in any detail. It was in discussing how to
elicit a whole sequence of such reminiscences that the
idea of marrying them to the basic London character

of the magazine first occurred, was received with delight by myself, and set in operation, before coffee had
been served, by the extraction from Mr Plomer of a
promise that he should write the first.

Once Mr Plomer's contribution was actually on my
table, I felt justified in inviting other writers to follow
on. My aim was to have contributors from every
generation or age-level, so that the series should eventually give an impression in movement, of an intellectual
scene gradually changing over four or five decades; how
much it remained the same in spite of the passing of
time was one of the questions I hoped the series would
answer. I also tried to assort my contributors, so that a
multifaceted picture might be built up, of literary
London as it appeared to newcomers approaching it
through various ports and sallies; London (unlike Paris)
being a conglomeration of villages even in the intellectual sense, it seemed to me quite possible that two people
of the same generation might give almost entirely different pictures, with scarcely any overlap between them.
The choice was not always easy; nor were the invitations
always accepted. Some authors (such as Mr W. H.
Auden) complained that they never had in fact 'come to
London' in the relevant sense of the words. Others
(such as Mr Stephen Spender) had already written as
much as they wanted to write on the subject in their
published memoirs. The disappointing refusals of one
or two who were asked were counterbalanced by the
welcome gate-crashings of others as time went on. In
fact the series gathered impetus, and has only come to
an end, which may well be but temporary, in order that

Mr John Baker might fulfil his agreeable plan of making
a book out of it.

Now that these fourteen contributors are all assem-
bled together, the first general reflection that occurs to
me is that London intellectual life is indeed, as Miss
Bowen suggests, 'multi-cellular', but that writers as a
whole have managed to be free of several cells at the
same time, so that cells have seldom, if ever, been completely isolated from one another. Miss Bowen herself,
for instance, moved in the circle of *The London Mercury*
and the circle of *The Saturday Westminster*; and, though
a little later, of Bloomsbury as well. In Lady Ottoline
Morrell's salon, to take another example, denizens of
the Bloomsbury 'cell' met denizens of *The London
Mercury* cell, as well as such distinguished figures as
W. B. Yeats, who did not belong to either. Perhaps
even more significant than that is the impression I have
of a surprising degree of continuity between the genera-
tions. Mr Leonard Woolf, for instance, describes how,
through getting to know Leslie Stephen, he was enabled
'to catch a last glimpse of that incredibly ancient London
literary world of ladies and gentlemen which went right
back to Thackeray and Dickens, to Mr and Mrs
Carlyle, to Mill and Huxley. It was the world of the
Quarterly and *Fortnightly* and *Cornhill*.' This would be
a fascinating observation from anyone—how much one
would have liked the theme to be developed—but it is
immensely more fascinating because Mr Woolf himself
was one of the original members of that Cambridge
constellation of outstandingly gifted thinkers, writers
and artists which later came to be known, on its

transference to London, as Bloomsbury; because it was through The Hogarth Press, founded by Mr Woolf with Leslie Stephen's daughter, that Mr Plomer tells us he made his earliest contact with literary London—as many others, including myself, have done since. Nor is it likely that this particular lineage will end there.

Literature appears to thrive best on a balance between the opportunities of solitude and the opportunities of gregariousness. The gregariousness is of the utmost importance if mind is to strike fire off mind, if ideas are to circulate and invention to be refreshed. 'Life in London,' says, on the one hand, that uncompromising protagonist of solitude, Mr Jocelyn Brooke, 'tends progressively to inhibit the creative faculty', while Mr J. B. Priestley, lauding the evening parties of thirty years ago, claims that they 'made something like a literary society possible. They enabled young writers to meet, on easy convivial terms, their distinguished elders. . . . This encouraged a healthy feeling of continuity in letters. It helped to banish those peculiar and often morbid notions that young writers cherish in loneliness'. Salons, indeed, or regular parties presided over by some host or hostess who had both zest and discrimination, appear to have provided one of the chief opportunities of meeting and discussing with other authors in London during the last half century, to judge from what the contributors to this volume tell us; next to them, editorial offices under the guidance of some exceptional figure who cared as much about bringing authors together as getting the paper out, and book shops where commercial ends had been all but lost sight of in the pleasures of intellectual life. Writer after writer pays tribute to the famous *Saturday Westminster* under the editorship of Miss Naomi Royde-Smith, evoking the temperate zone it created around itself for young poets and for novelists in need of reviewing guineas. Miss Rose Macaulay writes: 'Naomi Royde-Smith was the centre of a lively and able circle of friends. Like Mrs Montague, the queen of the blues, she did not encourage idiots. With her, I met, in this pre-war golden age, a number of people who seemed to me, an innocent from the Cam, to be more sparklingly alive than any in my home world.' The same impression, of brilliant talk and effervescing ideas is given by Mr J. B. Priestley of the office of *The London Mercury* under Squire: 'There, every week-day between twelve-thirty and two, was a gathering of wits who produced the liveliest talk I ever remember hearing.' (What has happened to all the witticisms that sparkled in those two circles?) Mr Priestley is not alone in having found *The London Mercury* a stimulating focus of talk and creative activity; and Mr Pryce-Jones has described its workings for us with a teasing affection, a world that was separate from Bloomsbury and separate from the world of the Sitwells, as well as from the world of Belloc, Wells and Bennett, though 'day by day, to the Temple Bar, emissaries from these different worlds came amicably together.' The magnet-pull of the Poetry Bookshop under Harold Monro seems to have been as great as, if not greater than that of these famous editorial offices. The readings organized there are celebrated by Miss Rose Macaulay, Miss Elizabeth

Bowen, and Mr William Plomer; and if Mr Geoffrey Grigson can remember being prevented by Monro from spending thirty-five shillings on Doughty's *The Dawn in Britain*, Mr George Barker remembers meeting Mr Grigson 'like a feline mandarin in shadows' in that well-known haunt of the younger poets of the thirties, Mr David Archer's bookshop-cum-publishing business off Southampton Row. Such places which attract the writers and artists of their time, various as they are, have one factor in common: a directing personality who loves books, pictures, people.

Writers, of course, are not only charting the literary history of our age in their reminiscences: they are also revealing themselves, and to many readers this may be their most interesting aspect. No glosses of mine are called for in this connexion; but I cannot help noticing what a strange proneness new literary stars have to arriving at parties in the wrong dress. Mr Leonard Woolf, for instance, arrives with Virginia Woolf, at what they find to their dismay to be a formal dinner of twelve or fourteen distinguished writers all in full evening dress, 'dirty and dishevelled from printing in the basement'; Mr J. B. Priestley and his friend Edward Davison, the poet, 'wearing tweeds and muddy walking shoes' find that a party to which they are invited by the Lynds is not an informal affair of drinks but 'most of literary London in full evening dress'. The likelihood of such gaffes is diminished today by the extreme *un*-likelihood of 'most of literary London' having full evening dress to put on; they will not occur in any companion volume to this that may be published in twenty years' time.

Finally, I believe these reminiscences may fascinate by their glimpses of a vanished London that had nothing to do with the dreams, ambitions and junketings of literary folk; glimpses that suddenly remind us what an unfair advantage in the struggle against oblivion the tiny, brilliantly lit literary circles in all their multicellular activity have, compared with the vaster and far more variously multicellular life of the metropolis beyond and all round them—precisely because they are inhabited by people with pens in their hands.

William Plomer

AFTER travelling across Siberia from the Far East, and after staying for a while both in Moscow and Warsaw, I had, by way of Berlin, reached Ostend. The winter of 1928–9 had been more than usually emphatic, and although it was, I think, already April and the sun was shining, a wind which had also lately crossed Siberia did not make the crossing to Dover an enticement.

It was still early in the morning, and the prospective passengers, congregated in the open air just before embarkation, were not in a jovial mood. I noticed that we were a mixed lot, by no means all English, and that among us was a tall Englishwoman with a figure like a cricket bat—straight, narrow, flat in front and only slightly convex at the back. Her tweeds, her long shanks and feet, her managing nose, and her inevitably prominent teeth would have made her splendid raw material for some virulent German or French cartoonist of the Boer War period. Her supercilious yet carrying voice was in keeping. It had in it more than a hint of arrogance, as if it were trying to convey that her position in life was so assured—racially, socially, and economically —that she had no need to worry about her want of feminine grace. One might fairly have classified her as an upper-middle-class ungentlewoman. After glancing

13

round at the closed, bluish, resigned faces of the other passengers, she said to her male companion (possibly a son or nephew) in an ineffably condescending drawl, pitching her voice so that we could all hear her:

'Everybody has an expression as if they were just going to take the first fence.'

This was no doubt her idea of a *bon mot*. It was in its way true, and issuing from some jolly, saddle-bashing riding-mistress, it would have been harmless enough. But it did not seem harmless to me. It seemed as if she wanted us all to know that the language of the hunting field was natural to her, and that if it was not natural to us, so much the worse for us, whatever we were.

Anybody may make some casual remark, in keeping with his nature and without harmful intention yet liable to make a bad impression when overheard. The bad impression made upon me on this occasion throws quite as much light upon me as upon the utterer. Being young, I was (I hope) suitably intolerant, but she had struck more of a chill into me than the east wind. I must try and explain why.

One of the effects of having left England when very young and of having been long absent was that although I came back with many pleasant memories of English people, places and things, I did come back a displaced person. I now understood, as I could not otherwise have understood, something of the strangeness a foreigner approaching England for the first time might feel, especially if he lacked the comforts of a settled background, substantial capital, and secure prospects. Such a foreigner, even if unprejudiced, might feel some appre-

hension about the English character and some of the
traits he might have heard attributed to it. I for my part
harboured disagreeable memories of a certain English
attitude to life against which I had from early childhood
been in rebellion. And now that I had sometimes seen
this attitude disagreeably exposed abroad, to the detri-
ment of our national reputation, I was more sensitive to
it and less ready to make allowances for it than before.

As a child I had perceived though I could not then
have defined this attitude. The adults I then liked least
were certainly complacent, insular, and hypocritical.
Any but athletic pleasures enjoyed by other people or by
the young were liable to incur their disapproval and
vindictiveness, and their ignorance of the non-British
peoples of the world was tinged with contempt. Such
types, residual from the Victorian era, are not yet ex-
tinct. In the lady of the first fence I had recognized
instantly a female of the species. Each of us might have
tickets to London, but my destination was quite different
from hers. Her London would have been more alien to
my temperament than some of the remote places I had
known, than Hluhluwe or Noboribetsu.

I think that after arriving in England I must for some
time have retained the formal and I suppose defensive
manners to which I had become accustomed when living
with the Japanese. I may also have brought with me
some traces of protective colouring.

'You've come back with a golden face,' my mother
said as soon as she saw me.

Going about without a hat in Japan may have given
my naturally anything but sallow skin a tinge of the

local complexion. My eyes were not slanted 'at ten to two,' as they say, nor had they developed the epicanthic fold, but they were sometimes as surprised at what they saw as Japanese eyes might have been. I remember for instance noticing with astonishment how well dressed English working men and girls were. They did not seem to be wearing working clothes at all. Were they now part of a one-class middle-class nation? As a child I had caught glimpses of ragged tramps, barefooted urchins, and drunken viragoes. I saw none now.

I continued my habit, then quite uncommon, of not wearing a hat, and some allusion being made to this at a luncheon party in London, an amiable man next to me said, 'Oh, but don't you think it looks a little *shoppy* to go about without a hat?' I was puzzled by this until he explained that he meant *like a shop assistant*. I said it had not occurred to me, and I should not really mind much if I were mistaken for a shop assistant. I may say in parenthesis that he died a year or two later of pneumonia brought on in winter at his wife's funeral. Instead of standing bareheaded by the grave he would have been wiser not to have taken off his hat. It may be necessary to suffer in order to be beautiful, it is hardly necessary to die for having taken the risk of looking like a shop assistant.

Many people expect a writer to look like the image they have formed of him in their own minds. I had hardly set foot in England before somebody or other exclaimed, 'Oh, but you don't look in the least like your books!' or, 'You don't look at all as I imagined you!' Several times since then strangers have come up to me

and begun a conversation, mistaking me for a doctor—
each time a different doctor—and once I was congratulated on my successful treatment of a difficult case of
hydrocele. I have thought these mistakes gratifying,
because a doctor may be expected to have some insight
into human nature and some powers of diagnosis, prog-
nosis, and analysis. I remember however that at the
time of which I am writing I was said by a painter to
look like 'a mixture of Puck and Buddha', so I suppose
my evident but unconsciously acquired Eastern aspect
was enlivened by gleams of Western playfulness.

Having arrived in England I went to spend the summer with my parents in a house far enough from London
for nightingales to be heard in the garden but not too
far to prevent my dining in London and returning home
by a late train. I was writing my second novel, and when
it was finished I moved to London. What were my
motives? First, the need to function as a writer, and to
exercise and develop whatever talent I might possess,
in what seemed at that moment the best environment.
Next, curiosity about people and about London itself,
and the impetus to unlock a London of one's own. Also,
the need to earn a living. Those three main motives are,
I believe, in the truthful order of precedence.

Looking back, I am mildly surprised at my unworld-
liness. I had no responsibility to contribute to the sup-
port of others, no intention of marrying, and almost no
interest in trying to make more money than was needful
to keep myself clothed, fed, warm, and clean, and to
perform such small acts of charity or present-giving and
make such modest returns of hospitality as might be

C.T.L.—B

possible for an indigent bachelor. I had no wish to impress anybody with my manner of living and felt no need to own or use many of the things that many people find indispensable, like a telephone, a car, or a club. I had not the faintest ambition to write best-sellers: it would never have occurred to me that my cast of mind was at all fitted to engage the interest of a large public. I have never been pushful, and would not have dreamed of soliciting any kind of favour or help from the eminent or the rich, from relations or friends, or of asking for any kind of job. Such ambition as I had lay entirely in the twin spheres of personal relationships and of literature.

I cannot pretend that I came to London a stranger. My family had had associations with it for at least four centuries, and I had myself often stayed there when young. I was now 25, and several years had passed since the publication in London of my first novel, the MS of which had travelled, I suppose, some six thousand miles to the Hogarth Press. I had also published two books of short stories, which, like the novel, had been well received—at least in some quarters. I had therefore in some respects more self-confidence than I should have had if I had not yet published anything.

I felt also some diffidence. What I almost wholly lacked, because when I had left England ten years before I had been too young to have formed any very close or settled or habitual friendships, were threads to take up, or a circle to re-enter. And yet for this lack, which displaced persons must expect, I was wonderfully compensated by friends luckily won by my earliest published writings.

For example, while living in Japan I had received a
fan-letter from an hotel in Sicily. It had been written by
an Englishman of about my own age, whose name was
new to me. He had understood or enjoyed what I was
driving at and had so warmly responded to my writings
that he wanted to make my acquaintance if I happened
to be about at any time. I wrote and told him that I had
arrived in England, we arranged to meet, and a friendship began which lasted until his death. He was a gay
and imaginative companion, not a writer, with a somewhat different experience of the world from mine, better
off than myself, extremely hospitable, and with a permanent family establishment in London, which became
almost like an extra home to me. Under his roof I first
met a variety of remarkable men and women, including
Paul Robeson, Walter Sickert and Julien Green.

I was no less welcomed by my publishers, Leonard
and Virginia Woolf, in those days established in Tavistock Square. To feel that they believed in me was much;
they had published my books; Leonard Woolf used to
send me other people's books for review in the *Nation*,
of which he was then literary editor; and soon after my
arrival they were good enough to invite me to the first
of a long series of evenings in Tavistock Square. Besides
enjoying their beautiful manners, incomparable conversation, and delicious food and wine, I was enabled to
meet there for the first time many persons of literary
distinction or unusual character, among them Lytton
Strachey, Lowes Dickinson, E. M. Forster, T. S. Eliot,
Desmond MacCarthy, Lady Ottoline Morrell, and
Hugh Walpole. About some of these I could find much

to say—but not just yet. However, as an indication of
the different levels on which it was possible for life to
go on a quarter of a century ago, I may say that Lady
Ottoline, without knowing it, occasioned one of the two
most old-world remarks I have ever heard. Far from
London an old noblewoman, hearing Lady Ottoline
praised as a patron of artists, said gravely, *'But she has
betrayed our Order.'*[1]

At Tavistock Square I sometimes met persons I had
met before. I remember Virginia Woolf being surprised,
when she introduced me to the beautiful Rosamond
Lehmann, that I knew her already. The discovery
aroused her characteristic and professional curiosity as
to *how, when* and *where.* Often writers of memoirs say
little about those curious links—like the movement in
the Lancers known as 'the grand chain'—by which
acquaintance is extended. I think I first met Rosamond
Lehmann through Stephen Spender, then still an undergraduate at Oxford; and Stephen Spender had been
brought forward by a Frenchman (once described as *'le
seul survivant du dixhuitième siècle'*) whom I had met
through my old friend, Laurens van der Post, at that
time living in London.

Through former friends and acquaintances at home
and abroad new perspectives opened every day. Each
day brought its own excitement, seeing John Gielgud

[1]The other remark is not strictly relevant, but seems worth
preserving in a footnote. A prince of a reigning royal house, having to move out of a small private room into a large hall where it
was his and his wife's duty to mingle with an expectant crowd of
respectable dressed-up citizenry and to make conversation with
them, glanced at a clock, took her hand, and said to her, 'Well,
come along, X., *it's time to charge the mob.'*

act, perhaps, or hearing Edith Sitwell read her poems; sitting to a sculptor, or being invited to contribute to a periodical; an old book, or a new face; a good idea, or a naughty caprice.

'Tell me, who's that?' I asked in a mixed gathering.

'That's Harold Monro,' said one of his contemporaries, and then called out to him in a teasing voice, 'Monro! *Miaow, miaow!*'

Monro turned, looked displeased, and said in a serious tone:

'That's a *good* poem, Z. That's a *good* poem.'

The allusion was to a poem of Monro's called 'Milk for the Cat', which in those days was widely familiar, and which had earned him a then surprising sum of money in anthology fees.

I looked at Monro with respectful curiosity. His own poetry had seemed to me like the voice of someone encaged or immured and trying in vain to get out: it is by no means all so gently domesticated and descriptive as the poem about the cat. As a boy at Rugby I had had 'rhyme sheets' from the Poetry Bookshop hung on my wall, best of all De la Mare's 'Arabia' with gaudy decorations by (I expect) Lovat Fraser: I still know it by heart. The successive volumes of *Georgian Poetry*, breaking in upon the post-Victorian twilight, had been as quickening to many of my generation, believe it or not, as a display of fireworks. I had lately visited the Poetry Bookshop for the first time, with its temple-like atmosphere and its polychromatic lining of 'slim volumes'. I should think better of London if it still had the Poetry Bookshop.

I think it true to say that I was far more interested in looking at pictures than in mixing with writers of my own age. I found it more useful and quieter and in general more pleasant. Having had to accustom my eyes to look at Chinese painting and the decorative arts of Japan, often with the utmost pleasure and admiration, I had for some time before leaving the Far East become aware that those eyes were starved for the sight of European painting. There is perhaps some significance in the fact that the painter who gave me the deepest satisfaction at this time in London was Poussin: those classical myths, those still, immortal gestures, those yellow draperies in some eternal-seeming golden light, nourished some impoverished appetite in me—but did not prevent me going round from gallery to gallery to see what was new.

When a young man comes to London the first question is whereabouts in London he is going to live. I should not have cared to live in Bloomsbury, architecturally pleasing though much of it was. In spite of my indebtedness to some of its more conspicuous denizens and my respect and growing affection for them I had no wish to be identified with anything like a movement, coterie, or literary school, however notable, and the word 'Bloomsbury' already had literary and often quite false and misinformed connotations. I did not care for the Thames-side climate of Chelsea, which I knew of old, nor for its new well-to-do floating population of Bohemian monkeys. Kensington was too sober, Mayfair too smart; and when I saw in some paper an advertisement of 'chambers near Hyde Park' I followed it up.

I envisaged one of those quiet, clean, comfortable, old-fashioned establishments not far from the Marble Arch, kept by some urbane ex-butler whose wife had been a housekeeper or lady's maid, in which when I was young my parents had sometimes taken rooms on short visits to London. I was quite mistaken. Imagination could hardly have allowed for what lay in hiding beyond that advertisement.

The house was in Bayswater, to which I was not at all disinclined. My grandparents had lived in Bayswater, my parents had been married there, and in 1918 I had tottered light-headedly out of a Bayswater nursing-home after recovering from the Spanish influenza. Besides, Bayswater in 1929 was not gloomy and decayed as it was in 1949: the Victorian age—called Edwardian in its last phase, which lasted until 1914—and the after-glow of Victorian prosperity had not yet wholly faded. Lest I be accused of trying to revert to the past, let me say that I did not hanker for it but was pleased or amused by what was left of it. I was pleased and amused by the aspect of the house now calling itself 'chambers'. Externally it was eighteen-sixtyish, villa-like, not tall and gaunt but with a cheerful light stucco façade, some pretty leafage inside the heavy iron gate, and its front door approached by a flight of welcoming and dignified steps under a projecting glass roof. Inside it had an air of spaciousness, bareness, and improvisation: I saw that it was scantily furnished. I took at once to the lively and pretty young Jewess who received me and explained that she was only just opening up the house. She made some passing allusion to her husband, but he did not

materialize. I took a large unfurnished room on the first
floor with a bathroom adjoining it and with a view of a
roseate Sweden-borgian church; I furnished it with a
bed, a desk, and other necessary things, and arranged
for breakfasts and for other meals if I wanted them. I
had come to London.

From a literary point of view it turned out to be no
disadvantage to me that the Jewess's husband was a
homicidal maniac. An equivocal character, he was alleged
to have some Mexican or American Indian blood. His
delusional insanity expressed itself in various ways, its
mainspring being a jealous suspicion of all other men in
relation to his wife, particularly those within a radius of
several miles, of course including myself. The greater
their propinquity, the greater his agitation. When it
reached a climax one November night he butchered her
in the presence of their child, and would, I was later assured, have butchered me in my sleep if I had not happened to
be away for the weekend. Beginner's luck, again, for me.

I did not immediately quit the house, as I had invited
some guests to a party there a week or two later and
there seemed no reason for putting them off. Soon after
the party I moved to an obscure dwelling in a mews. It
had character, and was called 'The Boreen' (Irish, I was
told, for a lane), but the French friend to whom I have
already alluded nicknamed it *'une ténébreuse affaire'* after
the story of that name by Balzac. I was not there long.
Early in 1930 I was invited to go on a rather grand tour
of Europe, to be followed by a sojourn in Greece. I
accepted the invitation, and my six months of acclima-
tization in London were over.

After a year or two I wrote a novel based on the circumstances of the crime. It had some success and was chosen by the Book Society, then a fairly new institution. If, when coming to London, I had not taken an independent line of action and if I had not settled in those 'chambers near Hyde Park' I should not have learned, or learned so soon, a good deal about people that I did learn, and I should not have been able or inclined to write that particular book, the work of a displaced person in a houseful of displaced persons. Accordingly if I were asked by a young literary aspirant what to do when coming to London, I might think that if he did not know what to do his aspiration could not be very purposeful, but I should perhaps suggest to him (arguing from my own experience) that a domestic life based in a non-literary and experimental environment *might* be more useful to him than going into a huddle for twenty-four hours out of every twenty-four with half-baked would-be littérateurs in bars, studios, clubs and beds: or it might not. I think I would also say that he might take and even cultivate opportunities of consorting with his elders and betters as well as with his coevals.

My present opinion is that London has become hardly fit to live in, that life in large cities may be over-stimulating to the young, and that frequent inhalations of fresh air help to counterbalance the mad metropolitan lures, and the insidious scurrying, noise, and dirt.

In conclusion I may say that I was to some extent in the confidence of the young woman who was murdered. Even more in her confidence was a cousin of hers, now also dead. He was a well-known and I hope singularly indiscreet consultant in Harley Street, who some time later chose to tell me the secret horrors of the poor woman's life. I think, on the whole, they can well remain among the many things I do not choose to write about, but I intend to allow the specialist himself a reappearance in my pages. In the vast human comedy of London in the nineteen-thirties, to which I had had such an irregular introduction, his fortunes were clandestinely linked, as in some sinister Balzacian invention, with those of a variety of men and women.

Leonard Woolf

I 'CAME TO LONDON' embryonically, I presume, in February 1880, for I was born in the West Cromwell Road on November 25, 1880, and I have lived in London—except for seven years in Ceylon—ever since. Thus I am a Cockney born and bred, and to ask me to recall my first impressions of coming to London or any segment of it is like asking a humble herring to recall his first impressions of coming to the sea. I have lived in Kensington, Putney, Bloomsbury, Fleet Street and Westminster, and they have left the smell of London (including Gower Street station on the Underground 60 years ago) in my nostrils and its strange, austere, homelike spirit in my bones. I love it profoundly and, as with all real love that goes deep into the entrails, I hate it profoundly.

One of the things which I have been asked to deal with in this article is my 'first impressions of the London literary world'. My feelings towards that world are probably also ambivalent. It is sometimes represented as composed of literary personages, major and minor, endless talking, eating, and drinking in pubs and Soho restaurants, in rooms and flats and parties. Into that world, if it exists, I have not penetrated, and I can only remember two occasions upon which I felt that I was in

27

the real London literary world, even though not of it. The first was when, latish in life, I was sometimes invited to the Sitwells, a dinner, say, with Osbert Sitwell or a party given by Edith Sitwell to meet Gertrude Stein. This was, of course, not in the least like the imaginary world of literary personages in Soho, but it was a literary world into which I went as an intruder feeling the inferiority complex of the amateur minnow among the great, confident, professional pike. To be led up to Gertrude Stein sitting on a kind of throne and to be given five minutes' conversation with her was what an old Edinburgh Writer to the *Signet* used to call 'an experience'. When he took me as a boy to see Abbotsford and halted me outside to survey that fantastic monument of literary fame and success, he said: 'This is an experience which ye'll do well to remember—O Ay, an experience ye'll do well to remember.' Gertrude Stein, I felt, was the same kind of experience.

My only other memory of entering the real London literary world recalls a more trivial and to me discreditable experience than a Sitwell party. Virginia and I accepted an invitation to dine with a well-known novelist whom we liked very much. We expected to dine with her alone or at most another guest, and late, dirty, and dishevelled we dashed from printing in the basement in a taxi to her flat—and found ourselves in a formal dinner of twelve or fourteen distinguished writers all in full evening dress. I suppose it was nervousness which made us fail the entrance examination to literary London. At any rate first, when one of those curious collective silences suddenly fell upon the company, Virginia's

extremely clear voice was heard to say: 'The Holy
Ghost?' to which the distinguished Catholic writer
sitting on her left replied with indignation: 'I did not
say Holy Ghost; I said the whole coast.' Almost immediately after, thinking that the distinguished lady writer
sitting on my left had dropped her white handkerchief
on the floor, I leant down, picked it up, and handed it to
her, to find, to my horror, that it was the hem of her
white petticoat which had protruded below her skirt. As
soon as we decently could, we slunk off home, feeling
that we had both disgraced ourselves in literary London.

Very different was my first meeting with a real
literary personage. It was in a barber's shop and I must
have been about 15. When I was 12 my father died and
my mother no longer affluent, moved with her nine
children to a house in Putney. One day I was having my
hair cut in a shop near Putney station and Putney Hill
when the door opened and everyone in the shop, includ-
the man cutting my hair, turned and looked at the person
who had come in. A tiny little man in a black cape and
a black sombrero-like hat, below which hung lank curls,
stood in the doorway. I had a sharp feeling of the fear
and pain in his pale-blue eyes and pallid face. He stood
silent in the doorway and looked at us and all of us
looked at him. He turned and went out, and, as he shut
the door, the hairdresser, beginning again to snip at my
hair, said: 'That is Mr Swinburne, the writer; he lives
at The Pines round the corner.' Swinburne, of course,
lived with Theodore Watts-Dunton, the author of
Aylwin, at The Pines, at the foot of Putney Hill, and
could be seen occasionally walking up to Wimbledon

Common and stopping now and then to kiss a baby in a
pram. Our doctor, who was a famous rugger international half-back, was also Swinburne's doctor; he told
me that when he was summoned by Watts-Dunton to
come and see the poet, Swinburne could rarely be induced to say a word to him; he would sit very upright in
a rather high chair and continually play an inaudible
tune with his two hands on the polished dining-room
table. The only other literary personage whom I met in
those days was Compton Mackenzie, but he had not yet
written anything and I had no idea that he would; we
were both at St Paul's and I first met him in a football
scrum on a cold wet November afternoon. We have
often met since in much more pleasant and more literary
surroundings. He once told me that I am included as one
of the characters in one of his *Four Winds of Love* novels.

In 1894 I managed to win a scholarship and entered
St Paul's School, where, under the highmastership of
the savage and eccentric Mr Walker, the engines of
education were applied violently and strangely to our
tender minds. As classical scholars and potential winners
of classical scholarships at Oxford or Cambridge, we
were treated like Strasbourg geese, except that instead
of being stuffed with food in order to fatten our livers,
our minds were stuffed for eight or ten hours every day
with the grammar, syntax, language and literature of
ancient Greece and ancient Rome. No educational training and regimentation of the human mind could be more
drastic, more ruthless than that to which we were subjected at St Paul's between the ages of 14 and 19, and
when I went up to Trinity College, Cambridge, in 1899,

I had an astonishingly thorough knowledge of the classical languages and literatures. And yet, though we spent
so many hours every day in the study of some of the
greatest literary masterpieces which have ever been
produced, interest in or even recognition of literature as
literature or of 'the arts' was certainly not in general
encouraged. The mental atmosphere was eminently
English, a kind of chastened and good-tempered barbar-
ism, a contemptuous Philistinism, based upon a pro-
found, devout veneration of the art of playing cricket or
football and distrust of everything connected with the
mind and intellect. Up to the age of 16, though my mind
was, I think, eager and active, I lived intellectually in a
trance, dimly aware that the pleasure I got from books,
literature, even work was vaguely discreditable and
should be concealed from my companions and teachers.

At the age of 16 I escaped from this land of the
Philistines and its dim intellectual twilight with the help
of one of the masters, A. M. Cooke, who was the
brother of a distinguished journalist, E. T. Cook,
editor of the *Daily News*. Cooke was a civilized, cultured, kindly, disillusioned schoolmaster, and an admirable teacher of the more intelligent boys. When I got
into his form, he liked my English essays and got into
the habit of walking round the playground with me
during the 'breaks'. He talked to me as to an equal,
sometimes about life and people, but more often about
books and writing. He encouraged me to believe that a
passion for great literature, even an aspiration to write
oneself, was not discreditable. Under his gentle stimu-
lation I read voraciously English and French master-

pieces, and one of the things which I am peculiarly grateful that he taught me was to combine with the highest standards of judgement the widest possible catholicity of appreciation and enjoyment. It was characteristic of him that he gave me as a personal parting gift when I went up to a higher form Bacon's *Essays* bound in pale-blue leather by Zaehnsdorf while approving my love of Borrow, and that he was eager that I should enjoy both Montaigne and *Tristram Shandy*.

It was largely due to Cooke that I had a wide acquaintance with and intense enthusiasm for literature when I went up to Trinity College, Cambridge, at the age of 18. Cooke himself had been practically the only outlet for my enthusiasm and for my eagerness to talk about books. It is true that in my last year I had the great honour of being invited to join a small debating society which met on Saturday afternoons in the houses of the members in rotation. It had been founded by G. K. Chesterton and his friends when they were at school, and Chesterton and E. C. Bentley, the author of *Trent's Last Case* and inventor of the clerihew, often came to our meetings. Bentley was then at Oxford and President of the Union, and Chesterton on the *Daily News* rapidly making a name for himself by his brilliantly paradoxical articles. But he and our society were passionately interested, not in books, but politics. I cannot remember ever discussing literature, but we had a 'mock parliament' and my recollection is of Gilbert Chesterton, a tall and at that time comparatively slim young man, making inordinately long, rather boring, Liberal speeches on local government, public houses, foreign policy, etc, and, as he spoke, tearing up sheets of paper into tiny pieces which he scattered on the table in front of him.

When I got to Trinity, I was astonished and delighted to find that among many of my contemporaries and seniors a love of literature and a desire to write books, intensive criticism and aesthetic speculations were accepted as natural and creditable for intelligent persons. Here for the first time I entered what might be called a literary world, a provincial literary world— even though it was Cambridge University—but which yet had connexions with the great metropolitan literary world of London. In 1899, a literary constellation of some brilliance or promise of brilliance centred in Trinity and King's. Among my seniors who were in residence as Fellows or frequently came up and stayed in Cambridge and whom I got to know well were George and Bob Trevelyan, G. E. Moore, Bertrand Russell and Desmond MacCarthy of Trinity and Goldie Lowes Dickinson and E. M. Forster of King's. Lytton Strachey and Thoby Stephen came up to Trinity in the same year as I did and through them I got a glimpse of an old Victorian London literary world which was just on the point of extinction. Thoby was the son of Leslie Stephen, the author of *An Agnostic's Apology, English Thought in the Eighteenth Century*, and *Hours in a Library*, editor of the *Dictionary of National Biography* and of the *Cornhill*. I met Leslie Stephen when he came and stayed with Thoby in Cambridge and again once or twice in London at his house in Hyde Park Gate. To a nervous young man he was, when one first met him, a

terrifying old man, for he was stone deaf and you had
to talk to him down an ear trumpet and his bearded face
looked as if it had been engraved for three score years
and ten with all the sorrows of the world; and when not
talking he occasionally groaned. In fact he was gentle
and kind and went out of his way to put us at our ease
and interest us. His talk enabled one to catch a last
glimpse of that incredibly ancient London literary world
of ladies and gentlemen which went right back to
Thackeray and Dickens, to Mr and Mrs Carlyle, to
Mill and Huxley. It was the world of the *Quarterly* and
Fortnightly and *Cornhill*. It died with Leslie Stephen and
John Morley, but later I met two relics or ghosts which
survived from it into our dishevelled age, Thomas
Hardy and Edmund Gosse.

Lytton was the son of Sir Richard Strachey, an
extraordinarily eminent, intelligent, cultured, amusing
Anglo-Indian soldier and administrator. When I knew
him, he sat all day long, winter and summer, in a large
chair in front of a large fire reading novels. Lytton's
mother, Lady Strachey, was a remarkable woman and I
came to have a great affection for her. She liked playing
billiards with me or for hours reading aloud to Lytton
and me masterpieces of English prose or poetry. In
their house in Lancaster Gate or some country house
which they took for the summer she would sit at the
head of the table around which her five sons and five
daughters together with a certain number of their wives
or husbands argued at the top of their Stracheyan voices
with Stracheyan vehemence. Lady Strachey seemed
entirely oblivious to or unaware of the terrific din. She

delighted to tell one about the vanishing literary world in which she had been the intimate friend of Lord Lytton, Browning and Tennyson.

In 1904 I went for seven years to Ceylon as a Civil Servant. The literary world of London faded far away into the background of my youth and my memories. Then in 1911 I came back on a year's leave and decided not to go back to Ceylon, but to settle in London and try to earn a living by writing. I found a London which motor cars and taxis and new building seemed to have changed fundamentally from the London of my youth. I went to live in Brunswick Square and there I found what I supposed has to be described as a new literary world. It came in time to be called popularly Bloomsbury. It consisted of Vanessa and Clive Bell, Roger Fry, Duncan Grant, E. M. Forster, Maynard Keynes, Virginia and Adrian Stephen, Lytton Strachey. We all wrote books or painted pictures and I sat myself down in Brunswick Square and wrote *The Village in the Jungle*. On Morgan Forster's advice I sent it to his publishers, Edward Arnold. It was accepted and published in 1913.

So I reached the goal set me by the editor for this article, my first publication and the London literary world of Bloomsbury. I do not propose to say anything about either, because, as Montaigne said so many years ago, it is not the goal, not the destination, not the arrival which is interesting, but the journey.

COMING TO LONDON: 3

V. S. Pritchett

THERE is a belief that when a young writer 'comes to London' he is at the decisive moment in his literary life. He meets other young writers; he becomes a member of a coterie or a set, perhaps; he meets the eminent, he is on the verge of success. This is true of many English writers, but it was not true of myself. As far as I can see, by comparing my life with the lives of my contemporaries, I was very late in meeting any writers at all in London; I met none of the eminent older figures and indeed had written nothing which would have deserved any notice from them. The development of what talents I have had has always been late and slow. I did indeed 'come to London' but I came there as an outsider and with a sense of bewilderment and personal defeat. It was the last city in the world I wanted to live in—a dulling, gloomy, friendless place it seemed to me. I remember getting off the Irish mail at Euston one early morning in the late twenties and going to a room which had been lent to me in Charlotte Street. It smelled of mice, tea leaves and stale gas. I was elated by travelling but I was scared.

I was 27 or 28 at the time and since I was 20 I had not lived in England. I had been brought up in London. First of all when I left school I had worked in the

leather trade at Bermondsey; then I had gone to
France and worked in a photographers off the Boulevard
des Italiens in Paris; later I had been a commercial
traveller selling glue and shellac to the ironmongers,
furniture makers and sealing wax manufacturers there.
I also sold—or rather, failed to sell, ostrich feathers
and became a temporary agent for theatre tickets.
All these occupations were ill-paid and boring. But
I read a lot and I wrote one or two sketches during
this time which were published in *The Saturday
Westminster, Time and Tide* and *The Christian Science
Monitor*, a very civilized American paper whose London
manager, an Englishman, I will call him Bassellthorpe,
had been infected with American impulsiveness. He
sent me to Ireland to write articles for his paper at
the time of the Irish Civil War. This was excellent for
me but reckless on his part for I was ignorant of Irish
politics and had never written a news article in my life.
After this I became a correspondent of the paper—and of
The Manchester Guardian—in Spain and North Africa,
travelled round the Mediterranean and went to the
United States. But the *Christian Science Monitor*,
though not a religious paper, had peculiarities which
were stultifying if one was interested, as I was, not in
politics but in art and in life. I did not wish to be a newspaper correspondent and the Americans, who tire of
things so quickly, were tired of me. I wanted to write
stories and novels and here they gave me more encour-
agement than I had ever received in England; partly
because it is natural for Americans to think that all
wishes are desirable and possible, partly because they

are egotists and wish to be shut of one as soon as is decently possible.

My arrival in London was really a return. I had been brought up there. It was a defeat, also. For it meant the end of a youthful vow I had made when I was 20, which was to travel, even emigrate and never to live in England again. The atmosphere I had been brought up in was extremely hostile to the intellect and the arts and the gulf which separated a young man of my background from the literary world seemed unbridgeable. If I had had a job or money at this time, I certainly would not have returned but necessity forced me to do so. The odd thing was that I knew more about the Irish, Spanish and American literary worlds than I knew about the English. I had listened to Yeats and AE, to Ortega y Gasset and to Unamuno; I had met clever young people in Boston and New York; but I was so ignorant of London life that I had no idea that Charlotte Street and Fitzroy Square had any connexion with the Bloomsbury group and did not even know that the group existed, until a London American told me about it. I had of course written nothing that would have attracted the interest of any circle of writers, beyond two awkward short stories one of which was published in the *Cornhill Magazine*; and I would have felt a hopeless shame and inferiority if I had met any of the Bloomsbury figures. Later on I was to discover that there was another barrier: they had leisure and I had to earn my living somehow. I had not leisure for the cultivation of personal relationships. Some of my friends tell me that I was lucky to grow up in circumstances so intellectually lethargic and out of touch, for, they say, one is thereby forced to 'live' first before writing. I enjoy 'living'—or is it indolent drifting? It is a puzzle to know how much a writer needs to 'live'. He needs a certain capital of 'life' and he needs to refresh it at intervals for the rest of his days by not doing any one thing too long. But 'living' is a matter of inner capacity and imagination. One can easily stagnate in 'living'; it is just as easy to avoid 'living', to lose the capacity because one has lost heart, in the midst of life, as it is in the favourable and closed worlds of literature and the arts. By the time one is 21 one has lived one life intensely; by 30, several other lives. The discipline and stimulus of other minds of the same bent is indispensable to writers, and they waste valuable time if they miss it. I have said earlier that it took me a long time to learn to write and although I had a talent for writing stories I would have written better ones earlier if I had lived among people who were informed and critical. I would not have muddled along in the conceited, day-dreaming and isolated way I had fallen into.

And so, knowing no writers, I fell back upon the only person I knew: the un-strange and monumental Mr Bassellthorpe. He was the manager of the American paper which did not now employ me and which, I saw, would have a fatal effect upon my prospects if it did. The fatality would have been double; first, because of the paper's policy and, second, because—like a large number of newspapers—it really regarded commentary on literature as a high class and even superior substitute for literature itself. The tendency to make literature

safe for its public is general in journalism and most
original writers have to battle with this evil which is all
the more insidious for being unconsciously promoted.
One might test writers by their resistance to the disease
—a drastic test which I myself would certainly come
very poorly out of.

The situation between Mr Bassellthorpe and myself
was an awkward one. He had seen some talent in me. I
was grateful to him. But we were—it was obvious to
both of us—parting company. He was kind enough to
want to hold on; I was anxious to go. We neither of us
could manage it. He was a very tall, solid, good man
in his sixties, generous, heavy in utterance and culti-
vated. Although English he had been Americanized
against his will—for he disliked Americans—and he had
one of those heavy bland transatlantic faces which became puddingy when he was morally disapproving. He
dressed very well, with the general air of being got up
for a funeral, a wedding or the Stock Exchange. He
greeted one with a clean, warm, brotherly smile which
contained a threat of authority and a smirk of embarrassment, his handshake was soft and engulfing and he wore
button boots. Like most young men I was scornful,
terrified, grateful, but driven to evasiveness by him.

The button boots of Mr Bassellthorpe were gentlemanly. They were contemptuously out of fashion, an
overpowering assertion of the authority of his generation. This came out even more strongly in the way he
quietly conveyed his wealth and his knowledge of the
world. He was a manager, but he conveyed that he sat
in his office out of a sort of *noblesse oblige* to public affairs

which he would modestly, but inexorably guide in a
gentlemanly way. But the most powerful impression he
gave was of boyish good health. At 60 he walked like a
Guardsman, and breathed the fumes of Piccadilly as
though they were nourishing. He became kinder, hap-
pier, stronger and more confident in physique and mind
every minute. This quality never became magnetic. It
did not communicate or travel. The better he felt, when
I called at his office or went to luncheon with him, the
less healthy I used to feel. I used even to get stomach
ache.

How, many years ago, Mr Bassellthorpe came to die
—and rather young too in the manner of American
businessmen—I cannot imagine. There was an odd kink
in him which, at any rate, made him disadvantageous as
the only literary mentor I had. He had given up literature. He had given it up on principle. When he was
young he had known all the writers: Wilde, Beardsley,
Conrad, Kipling, Shaw. He had known Yeats. He had
read widely and thoroughly but, I now think, with con-
descension and a majestic absence of enthusiasm. The
truth is that, suddenly, he had experienced religious
conversion. I do not know the circumstances. He had
become, perhaps because of his good health, a Christian
Scientist. He had come of Quaker stock and the humble,
artisan birth of the original disciples of Mrs Eddy in
the dreary town of Lynn in Massachussetts, gave a
moral cachet to his faith, as it did for the faith of many
of the smart and devout of Knightsbridge. This conversion made him look upon literature as a sad if once
delectable mistake, for the arts are concerned with evil

as well as good—and evil, according to this religion, did not exist. Now, he drank no wine, smoked no cigars, read no books. Yet he would like to remember these lost errors. He would recall vintages with nostalgia and books with puzzled regret. As a young writer whom he encouraged, I was his sin. He used to say how tragic it was that Dostoevsky had not lived in Mrs Eddy's lifetime for the Russian would have gained much from her works. Tolstoy, he thought, was nearer 'the Truth' despite his pride. It was mysterious, he found, that a great genius like Shakespeare should have written lines which fell short of the Bostonian ethic. Mrs Eddy thought so too. He hated the Irish on general Anglo-Saxon grounds, and once quoted a line from a Celtic poet —'What does the salmon dream?'—in the offended voice of one who had been told a downright lie. 'Salmons don't dream,' he said.

The imagination was Mr Bassellthorpe's difficulty: he had none. He hated sensibility: he despised the heart. His worst word of abuse was 'emotional'. This was enough to make our conversation one-sided; but there was another more awkward reason. I myself had been dipped into Christian Science when I was young; had dipped and lapsed, dipped and lapsed until I had finally lapsed altogether. Since to lapse was 'error' and error did not exist, I could never, in Mr Bassellthorpe's view, be said to have lapsed at all. I was in the false situation of one who is rescued from drowning by an over-earnest member of the Humane Society when he is not drowning at all. Sometimes idle remarks of mine drove the brotherly smile from Mr Bassellthorpe's face and I would feel an almost physical shock as if I had had a life-buoy thrown at me instead of for me. I remember an instance of this.

Like many cheerful Puritans who are free of the pleasures of the flesh, Mr Bassellthorpe excepted the pleasure of eating well. Since I was living poorly on the proceeds of translating business and technical documents at the rate of a farthing per English word I was glad to be taken to expensive restaurants by him. One day, as we went into one of these places, I told him that the stick I was carrying—it was one of my affectations, I thought all writers carried sticks—was a male bamboo. 'Beware,' said Mr Bassellthorpe, his face becoming like cold suet, 'Beware of getting sex on the brain.'

But Mr Bassellthorpe, though he disapproved, he was benevolent. He saw that I needed to be put on to editors who know more about the literary world than he did. He put me on to H. M. Tomlinson of *The Nation*, a writer I greatly admired and still do. I was shocked to find a tired man. Even more shocked to hear from him that I was a fool to try to be a writer in England and that I had better go back abroad as quickly as possible. The same answer came from Mr Garvin on *The Observer*. Mr Garvin's leading articles in that paper used to lie about my parents' house on Sunday mornings, like enormous eighteenth century tombstones. They stunned, as they were read, with their huge metaphors and their inescapable message of human fatality. Now I actually sat before Mr Garvin's desk. His head was hidden in his hands and he looked up at me with large, distraught eyes like someone coming round from

a migraine or like Irving reciting *The Bells*. His voice
moaned as he said that he was unable to tell me what to
do *now*. He could (he said) only speak of the future. He
lived in the future, two months, six months, years
ahead, in what was *going* to happen. I felt raw, shy and
topical. 'Don't stay here in London. Get away,' he said.
'South America. Nobody realizes,' he said, 'that in fifty,
a hundred, two hundred years' time it will be the most
important place on earth.' I felt I had only a short time
to live. I asked if I could review a book now. He was
rather short about this request.

'You must ask my daughter who sits over at that
window,' he said. 'Known, most formally, in his office as
Miss Garvin.' It was Miss Garvin's day off. I did not
return. I went back to Charlotte Street, to work at my
translations, to get on with a book I was writing, some
stories and an obituary notice of Primo de Rivera. Mr
Bassellthorpe's shadow was on me. He would hate my
book. He would loathe my short stories. I had heard
what he thought of Tolstoy.

But, as I have said, Mr Bassellthorpe loved bene-
volence. He said he knew a publisher, a Mr Hicks-
Flannell. My acquaintance with Mr Hicks-Flannell was
very short but one fact caught my eye at once. Like Mr
Bassellthorpe he wore button boots. Like him also he
was a Christian Scientist, and a gentleman of means. But
whereas Mr Bassellthorpe was well-dressed and quietly,
impregnably confident, Mr Hicks-Flannell was thin,
saturnine and melancholy. I do not think he had lost all
his money, but he had the fated look of someone dedi-
cated to the disappearance of the remains of a small

private inheritance. Put it in beer, put it in tobacco, one
wanted to say to him; but he was intended, by higher
powers than his own, for the undetectable leak, the
diminishing return. He had been in a silent way, in the
Navy, possibly had kept deep diaries. God would never
fail to answer the prayers of Mr Bassellthorpe. He
would just nod his head in acquiesence at the unassuming regularity of his views. Mr Hicks-Flannell's prayers,
I would guess, were treated parsimoniously simply
because they would be irregular and desperate, but he
took a refined pride in this negligence. He regarded his
merits as explicable disadvantages and, in other circumstances, might have become an ascetic or a priest. He
disliked the world. I cannot remember what he said to
me but there were curious remarks about the decline of
the arts, the commercialization of life, the tide of vul-
garity sweeping all before it, the smallness of hope and
something about the atmosphere being inappropriate
and the situation difficult. He glanced at an inner door
in his office when he said this as if the inappropriate
trapped us. From behind the door came the dilatory and
festive voice of the partner of Mr Hicks-Flannell. Irony
had got its claws into him: his partner's name was
Eddy. My manuscript came back rejected within a
week.

This did not surprise me. I had to re-write it all the
following year before any publisher would keep it any
longer than that. But many years later I met Mr Eddy
for the first time and Mr Eddy said, 'if he had only
known' he would have published me at once. 'Known
what' I asked. 'Well, if you had only not come through

Mr Hicks-Flannell.' 'What happened to Mr Hicks-Flannell?' I asked. 'Run over,' said Mr Eddy with some self-importance. It was almost as if he had arranged the accident. I saw that Mr Eddy had, with satisfaction, appointed himself to be the plague of Mr Hicks-Flannell's life. And with just cause. For Mr Eddy was angry. He had never forgiven *Christian Science* for being issued under the imprint of his own name, and he made Mr Hicks-Flannell responsible for the irritation. Mr Eddy was driven mad by the suspicion that Mr Hicks-Flannell's manuscripts had been considered in the spirit of prayer and it was his policy to smell out Mr Hicks-Flannell's prayers and squash them. I was one. Mr Eddy was a pale, round, obsequious man with a shrewd and psalmy voice but there was also an air of Brighton sea-front, Edwardian night clubs, pinching fingers and binoculars also. I can imagine him with a watering-can in his garden, but also peeping through a hole in the fence. He dropped from time to time a very friendly aitch. And so, from his confidences, I gathered his technique as a publisher. He waited for his partner to bring in a manuscript, say, about Greece; he suspected at once the infiltration of the hated religion. With a knowing smile he would immediately produce a much better book on Turkey and say innocently that the author was a very interesting man—a Methodist, a Catholic or a Buddhist, perhaps, a Spiritualist, a Theosophist. Mr Hicks-Flannell suffered for his faith. But not the firm; it made its money in the byways of electricity, soldering for beginners, the handbook trade and so on. The partners were united in their belief that

literature was in decline. My manuscript confirmed
them. Some other publisher took it.

Lucky for me, but unlucky for my friendship with
Mr Bassellthorpe. He had seen my progress and now
regretted it. I knew the sight of any book or story of
mine would be fatal to our friendship. I gave him a copy
of my book. He said with his usual kindness, 'Now you
are an author' and admired the binding. But when he
read this and one more of my books, he could not hide
his feelings. His face was heavy, hurt, the face of a dog
that forgives but cannot forget. 'Why,' he said, 'do you
write about the evil in people and not the good?' I said
I wrote as I saw and, no doubt, as I was. 'But couldn't
you try to be *better?*' he said. It was the end. The following day, good and earnest Quaker that he had been, he
wrote me a letter of apology. He had spoken in an un-
Christian manner, we must all follow our understanding.
The light was there for all to see. Alas, the damage was
done. Dostoevsky, Tolstoy, Yeats, we had all fallen
short. Misanthropically, but benevolent to the end, he
gave me a book to review for his paper.

I went shortly afterwards to my first literary party.
It was held in a small room and was packed with people.
I knew none of them. A gentleman in a tail coat said to
me 'This room is very hot.' Another said 'This room is
very high.' An elderly lady, told to be kind to me, asked
me what was the most exciting thing I had ever done in
my life and said *she* had swum over a volcano. I sank and
left the party. I had already spent the twenty pounds
advance on the book and was down to about nine
shillings. I went off to read the notices of Bodies

Found outside Scotland Yard. It was a very cold day.

More than 'coming to London', the return to England was the important thing for me and the slow renewal of contacts with English life. Sometimes I have lived in London, sometimes in the country, in both places with rewards and dissatisfactions. I have continued to travel, having had restlessness planted in me in early childhood. My family moved house, chiefly about London, fourteen times or more before I grew up, and we felt the excitement of new places and the illusion of saying 'At last, I could live here.' We never could. All writers are different, but I think all write out of the tensions inside themselves. No tensions, no writing. It is difficult to know what are the gains or losses of expatriation but, I think, I learned one very important fact which John Stuart Mill noted about England in his essay on *The Subjection of Women*; it is a fact which has always given a special difficulty to the English writer. Mill said that our strong sense of social discipline made it very difficult for us to be judges of the natural lineaments of human nature. I think going abroad for a long time helped me a little in looking at England with this veil removed. English people became foreign to me and that was an advantage, for it removed some of the drabness, the curtain of convention with which, very cunningly, we cover up what is really going on in our lives. There was another practical gain. When I went abroad with the intention of becoming foreign the project encouraged the cultivation of empathy, the attempt to divest oneself of oneself and to become the thing or person seen. In the long run my success in this was small, but the project did involve very attentive listening to the words people used in various languages in their conversation, and that has turned out to be a valuable and permanent interest to me as a writer of stories. All writers I have known have complained of periods of sluggishness and boredom in their minds. It is not until they suddenly see things, words, places, persons, situations as something else that their minds begin to wake up again. London became London to me when it became foreign.

George Barker

I

I FIRST came to London in a pram when I was 6
months old; I left it at the age of 13 when I rode
away to Wembley Exhibition on a ball-bearing scooter.
Nothing much happened in between except my elemen-
tary education and some infant essayings in the art of
love. But perhaps I do this time of my life an injustice,
for I poignantly recall that day of my ninth year when I
composed my first—and who shall say my last—poem,
which was a ten-page monstrosity in the stanza of *The
Faerie Queene* entitled 'The Tournament'. And that
other day, not long before I scootered away to Wembley, on which I opened my father's insurance ledger (it
was a large one, because at this time he was an insurance agent) to design an overlarge crypto-Renaissance
catafalque inscribed: Georgius Barca, 1913–1926.

So that I could more properly claim to have come to
London when, after two days, I returned from the Great
Exhibition to my home in Chelsea. And surely, in this
case, I am the first poet ever to have arrived in the
capital by home-made scooter? (These machines,
incidentally, were highly favoured by my contemporaries: they were constructed out of a road tar-block,
two spars of wood, two automobile ball-bearings as

wheels, and a meat skewer.) Then in 1925 I was over-
seen at school reading a book—this pastime was not
practised by any of the other thousand pupils—from
which I received what still seems to me to be the highly
distinguished monicker of Hadji. The book was that
novel by the one-time ambassador to Ispahan, Sir
James Morier.

II

But can such feckless recollections in any way re-
semble literary reminiscences? At 14 I sent a poem of
laudation to Lord Dunsany because I considered Francis
Ledwidge the best of the War Poets. At 15 I was
rigorously helping Mr James Joyce to finish what at
that time he called his *Work in Progress*. My childhood
came to an end on that day in nineteen hundred and
heaven knows what when I spent my lunch money on a
poem which seemed to me so great that for two or three
days afterwards my own poems disappointed me. I mean
'Ash Wednesday'.

For, really, what should be reminiscences of literary
people and literary occasions becomes, in my mind,
certain books and the eccentric consequences of reading
them. The *Son of Woman* so deeply moved me that I
sat down and in a week wrote what professed to be a
year's journal, which I pestiferously despatched to Mr
Middleton Murry. He invited me to tea with Sir
Richard Rees and gave me a little book to review for
The Adelphi: it was *New Signatures*. I shall always have
unpleasant recollections of this book because it had jam
on it. Mr Murry then wrote me a delicate note (of

'introduction') to present to a man whose named seemed to promise not much less than he himself fulfilled. I found myself in an empty room in Fitzroy Square awaiting the arrival of Michael Roberts. I sat for a long while. Then I got up, looked over the banisters, and saw a sweatered mountaineer ascending the staircase. This immensely impressive figure carried alpenstocks and spears and snowshoes and a whole paraphernalia of rods and instruments. When he entered the empty—or almost empty—room, I gave him the little note and he kindly gave me a bowl of macaroons. Then he went over to an old gramophone and put a record on. 'Just sit and eat the macaroons and listen to these,' he said, and handed me some more records. They were the quartets of Beethoven. (I tried to write a poem about this occasion.) 'I'm going to change,' he said. When he reappeared he was disguised as a literary physicist. 'Now let's talk,' he began, and proceeded to do so for hours and I sat so bemused that I could neither speak nor hear a word. This, properly, constituted my introduction to literary London. I was rendered invisible, inaudible and delighted by a bespectacled magician with a snake in his mouth. For I had never before and have not often since witnessed that glacial machine of transfigurations, the masculine intelligence, in its most brilliant operations. And in spite of or because of the fact that I have never been able to recall one word or idea he uttered, I know that his act of intellectual callisthenics left me with one very clear recollection: this was the ease and grace with which he forgave me for being there.

III

It was Michael Roberts who told me to look around the corner at a bookshop from which the *20th Century Magazine* was intermittently issued. But before doing so I took the reckless precaution of sending the editor one of my poems: I received in reply a note of invitation to call from a Mr David Archer, who was, I gathered from his notepaper, the proprietor of the bookshop itself. I called one clear and sunny morning, at about eleven o'clock, and entered a showroom in which bright books on Marxism and bright books of verse were unneatly displayed everywhere. Up a ladder in a corner the tall and elegant figure of a character who might have stepped equally well out of Wodehouse or Proust—or, more probably, both—this figure, crucified against the upper wall, turned to me with a look of despair and relief as I entered. Then it addressed me: 'Be an angel,' it said, 'hand me that hammer.' This was Archer, whose posture of crucifixion up a ladder has never forsaken him, and whose insight into contemporary verse helped to form the poetic opinion of a generation. He invited me to take coffee. We went across the street into a café full of overcoated poets and truant schoolboys. There was an atmosphere of industrious conspiracy and illegal enthusiasms. Mr David Archer was looking for a young poet to publish. Mr Grigson, like a feline mandarin in shadows, was preparing his first or second issue of blood, entitled *New Verse*. A dark young horse was pointed out to me as the bright hope of the new poetry; he had a sad ingratiating face and bore his responsibility with deliberation. This

was Mr Charles Madge, most gracious of poets. Somewhere else an elongated Blue Boy of 15 was preparing
to live down his recently published first novel. I can
never remember whether David Gascoyne really spoke
only in French at this time, or whether he merely
happened to give this impression.

IV

Then I got myself a job delivering books for a firm
by the name of the Janus Press; this enabled me to take
a little attic room in Westbourne Terrace. It seemed to
me admirable that I should write a successful novel and
move into a larger attic. I wrote the novel. It made no
money, but it did gain for me the friendship of Edwin
Muir, who, having written about the book, asked me to
call and see him at his house in Hampstead. I went one
wet evening in the autumn and met for the first time a
phenomenon I hope never to forget: the extraordinary
gentleness that prevails in the presence of many men
who are truly poets.

I think often with gratitude of evenings spent in his
quiet company, because here I learned that words were
not only delightful things in themselves but also—this
mysterious fact still fascinates me—that they stand for
far more than most people either think or are. Muir was
like a silent clock that showed not the time but the con-
dition, not the hour but the alternative.

And I as gratefully remember that occasion when the
overpowering caryatid of Willa Muir took up Homer
and began to recite that opening passage in the Greek,
so that the whole of the tasteful room in Hampstead

gradually filled with the loud-mouthed rolling parallels of the poem and the sea—until I was witnessing the living demonstration of Eliot's assertion that a poem can communicate before it is understood.

V

Colonel Lawrence sidling into Archer's Bookshop, toying with a cold cup of tea and then disappearing in front of our eyes like a Middle Eastern fakir. John Cornford, filthy and consumed with a ferocity of nervous energy, ashamed and delighted when it was disclosed that he had written the two beautiful poems published in *The Listener* under a Welsh pseudonym. A rubicund young sheep farmer from the hinterland of Australia who really did know the words and the tune that the fishy girls sang and how Achilles hid himself among women: I mean Albert Lancaster Lloyd, singer, scholar, whaler. And a small thin Dylan Thomas with a dirty wool scarf wound around himself like an old love affair, looking liker to a runaway schoolboy than Esmond Romilly, who really was one. The 20 year old matinée idol perpetually fiddling with a self conscious pipe, the critic and snake charmer Desmond Hawkins, explaining how he could never finish his novel because when he reached the last page the first one revolted him.

I do not know how many juvenile revolutionaries were temporarily harboured on the top floor of this bookshop, but they came and went like a rotation of furious tiger-moths, always at night. Mothers arrived, weeping, in taxicabs. Did all the conspirators die, I wonder, in Spain?

VI

There were the scalds and there were the heroes, almost none of them at the legal majority, milling frenziedly around the abstracted proprietor or impresario, David Archer, who could, with a single word, bring all these restless temperaments into an even more hysterical chaos of convulsive irresolution. If women and drink have saved many poets from madness and death, here, in Parton Street, politics and poetry saved many of us from women and drink.

When I was not taking my place in the complicated epicycles of friendship and jealousy at Archer's Bookshop, I was either in a cinema or a job or a museum. I fell in love with the Duchess of Milan in a black dress, with the heroic torsos of Mestrovic, with Kevin Barry, with Alexander Archipenko, with the Fantasia of the Unconscious, with all Middle English Poetry, with the idea of Italy, and with myself. This by no means exhausts the cauldron of my unholy loves. There were evenings under mackintoshes in Richmond Park, furtive exercises in experimental acquaintanceships at cinemas intimacies that lasted for seconds in ABC's, passionate familiarities with people who never knew it, and some who did: all the long, distraught and feverish searchings of the late adolescent at liberty in a great city, those searchings that only too often finish up at a mirror in a furnished room or in a dream of violence.

I haunted the Edgware Road and extemporized a susceptibility for waitresses; I sat down outside the Brompton Oratory to count those who entered and, finding there were seventy women to ten men, informally seceded from the Roman Catholic faith. For a firm in Clerkenwell Road I designed abominable wallpaper and for another in Holborn tested radio transformers. I lost most of these jobs (I had dozens) because the buses on which I went to work, by some providential coincidence, always passed by the National Gallery, and it seemed to me then and it seems to me now an unpardonable waste of time to test radio transformers or design bad wallpaper while great paintings, like dolled up women, wait to be admired.

As I see it now, this time of my youth was spent wandering around in always public places, parks, galleries, museums, gardens, streets, embankments, etc. One was pursuing, I suppose, that improbable stranger who will turn around and, without irony, recognize one as truly another person. Whereas, instead, there is only the inverted glare of the white collared worrier going home or the virtuous back of a mother pushing her second self along in a wheelchair to nowhere. What is it that the young man is flying from or flying into when he resorts to public places and I do not mean lavatories? It is, I suppose, whatever brings one to London.

VII

And so I wrote a harder poem about this kind of subject and showed it to Muir, who suggested that I should send it to Mr T. S. Eliot at the *Criterion*. This abashed me as profoundly as if he had suggested Mount Parnassus, but I did so. (I have never recovered from the surprised privilege of being alive at the same time as the man who wrote. 'Ash Wednesday'.) And that was how my *Poems* came to be published. So I got married and left London and went to live in a cottage where my address was: The Butts, Plush, Folly, Piddle-trenthide.

IT was in the early autumn of 1922 that I arrived in London, to live and work there. I had taken my degree at Cambridge the year before, and had also got married; but as my ex-officer's grant still had a year to run, I returned to Cambridge, to do some coaching in English and to write essays and reviews. Even by the May Term of 1922 I was still uncertain what I wanted to do—that is, to earn a living, for I meant to go on writing whatever else I might do. I refused the chances of several remote professorships, in places like Dorpat, partly because I could never discover what the salaries were worth in sterling, for no country whose currency was quoted in *The Times* wanted my services. I qualified, if that is the term, as a University Extension lecturer, by delivering a sample lecture to ten depressed working men and a large bored cleric in a Cambridgeshire village institute; and finally was told I had been appointed for the autumn session to the North Devon region. (A summary of a proposed Extension course, given to me as a model to copy, was the work of an older Cambridge man—one Forster, E. M.) Then dear old 'Q', whom I parodied in the *Cambridge Review*, suggested I should stay on to give some lectures in Eng. Lit., but I think I pleased him, and certainly annoyed the University Ex-

tension people, by suddenly deciding I would freelance
in London. So there I went, with a young wife, no
regular job, and a total capital of less than fifty
pounds.

We found a seven-roomed flat on the ground floor
of King Edward's Mansions, Walham Green, which
perhaps I ought to explain is a seedy district between
Chelsea and Fulham, their rather raffish poor relation.
The rent was about seventy-five pounds a year—and
ours was probably the roomiest flat in the building. But
for the first few months we shared the flat with our
Cambridge friend, Edward Davison the poet, who had
edited the *Cambridge Review* and now came to London
to edit a Liberal Church weekly called *The Challenge*.
We shopped sketchily for odd bits of furniture along the
Fulham Road, our one solid piece being a Broadwood
grand on hire purchase; we did out own decorating, half
poisoning ourselves with white lead; we settled in.
Many of our neighbours there were music-hall per-
formers, who were on tour most of the year and did not
want to pay much rent for a permanent address in
London: Walham Green would do. It would do for me
too; in fact, at first I quite enjoyed living there. I do not
know what it is like now, but in 1922 Walham Green
still seemed to belong to the London of Phil May. It
was crowded and noisy with street stalls and barrows,
fat women drinking stout at pub doors, young mothers
shouting at wizened babies, chaps waiting to learn what
won the two-thirty, greasy little eating-places; with the
Granville Music-hall and Stamford Bridge (where Davison and I cheered for Chelsea) representing the arts and

athletics. We were not long in Walham Green, leaving it for the Chilterns the following spring, and I will not pretend I was sorry to go; but for the first two or three months I certainly relished what seemed to me its thick Cockney atmosphere, very different from anything I had known in the North. To this day there is a certain kind of smoky autumn morning, coolish but with the sun somewhere not far away, with a railway station smell about it, that brings back to mind those first days in London, when I would hurry out of King Edward's Mansions to catch an 11 bus to Fleet Street, hoping to find some books to review.

I was already writing critical articles and miscellaneous essays, but I had to depend largely on reviewing, for which then there was ample space. Most daily papers carried at least one book page a week; there were far more bookish weeklies than there are now; and various monthly reviews and magazines were open to young writers. The pay was low, especially for unsigned short notices, but often these bulky volumes of travel and memoirs were fairly expensive, and we could sell our review copies at half the published price. The old fellow who bought them had one touch of genius: he always paid us in new pound notes, deliciously clean and crisp, and to be handed seven or eight of these was always an exhilarating experience, like being in a fairy tale for a few minutes. We used to hurry out of that shop, all Fleet Street ours, like Ali Baba out of the robbers' cave. It is, I think, the only money I have ever had that brought with it every possible good sensation of wealth. Even the faint feeling of guilt—for the publishers' and

booksellers' associations were for ever denouncing this
outrageous practice—only added its final flicker of zest,
a garlic touch of the disreputable.

All this reviewing, however, was fairly hard work,
even if, as I was, you were a fast skimmer and gutter of
books that did not pretend to be literature. To go
through a pile of them, for the purpose of sending in a
half-column of *Shorter Notices*, could be sheer drudgery,
especially if you were tackling the job at the end of a
day spent on your own writing. But I was more fortun-
ate than most new arrivals—or indeed many of the old
hands, for in those days there was in every Fleet Street
pub at least one man who earned a living of sorts out of
minor reviewing. During this first year I did regular
reviewing, mostly signed, for the *London Mercury*, the
Outlook, the *Bookman*, the *Daily News*, the *Daily Chron-
icle*. And a little later I wrote long signed reviews too
for the *Spectator* and the *Saturday Review*. I had little
difficulty with literary editors, although there were
plenty of us asking for books. This was not because I
was particularly wise or witty but because, unlike many
of my rivals, I took my reviewing seriously, bringing to
it a solid North-country conscientiousness; I never left
my review copies unread at studios where too much
cheap Chianti had been gulped down; I was always rea-
sonably on time; and I never delivered two hundred or
two thousand words when I had been asked for five
hundred. Again, even in those early days I never asked
for a book because I disliked its author and so wanted to
attack him; and I have kept to this rule. Anonymous
reviewing, a bad practice, has always particularly en-

couraged the 'stealthy assassins', and at no time have I
ever been one of them.

While I was still in Walham Green I became a publisher's reader, thanks to J. C. (now Sir John) Squire,
who had been asked by John Lane to recommend somebody for the job. I was paid about six pounds a week,
though I seem to remember this covered a certain
amount of editorial work, of which *The Bodley Head
Book of Verse* was one of the fruits. I spent only one
morning a week, generally Tuesday, in the offices in
Vigo Street, where I went through the manuscripts that
had arrived during the previous week, threw out the
obviously unacceptable, and put aside, to be sent home,
anything that looked at all promising. John Lane, who
died in 1925 at the age of 71, seemed to me much older
than he actually was; he had almost lost his sight and
appeared to move like a very old man; also, he was one
of the representative figures of a vanished era, at his
best as a publisher about the time I was born. As soon
as he was successful he must always have spent more
time lunching and dining out than he did in reading
manuscripts and books; nevertheless, he had a remarkable 'nose' for books and authors, not because he himself represented a new and growing public—he was not
like Dent or C. S. Evans of Heinemann (who almost did
more for Galsworthy than Galsworthy did)—but because he had a flair for knowing what book would get
itself talked about where he lunched and dined. He
moved easily and surely in the region, far more important in the 'nineties than it has ever been since, somewhere between literature and fashion. He was the dandy

among publishers—just the man to bring out Max
Beerbohm—though, oddly enough, he was the son of a
North Devon miller and spent his first eighteen years
in London as a clerk in the Railway Clearing House. (A
good-looking alert youth I used to run into at Vigo
Street had a better start. His name was Allen Lane.)
Like many old-fashioned publishers, John Lane would
spend money lavishly *on* an author, offering him some
of the best wines and brandies from the Café Royal
cellars, but disliked handing over money *to* the author;
so that his usual terms were shocking, with royalty
scales cut to the bone, thirteen copies counting as
twelve, and much jiggery-pokery with subsidiary rights.
This combination of parsimony with flair meant that
the Bodley Head had probably the best list of good *first*
books in town. The tradition still existed in my time.

If as a reader I missed anything first-class, success-
fully published elsewhere, I am unable to recall a single
example. What I do know for certain is that I recom-
mended—and without difficulty, because there was much
new talent about in those years—an impressive list of
first books and new authors, headed by Grahame Greene
and C. S. Forester. Perhaps my oddest find was a huge
Amazonian jungle of a manuscript, which after a great
deal of cutting and rearranging appeared as *Cubwood*,
with an introduction, at my request, from Walter de la
Mare. It was an involved and highly introverted account
of the adventures of some children in a wood, and was
the work, over years, of a fantastic old gentleman who
looked and was ready to behave like one of Emmet's
creations. Unless my memory is tricking me, he would

suddenly appear and disappear in Vigo Street, depositing with wool-mittened hands further and more involved instalments of his book, as if we were all in *Through the Looking Glass*. The story reads like an actual remembrance of childhood, recalled in great detail, yet in fact, he assured us, it was all an invention, the record of a dream life he had enjoyed for many years. In spite of Walter de la Mare's Introduction—'It is a visit,' he said, 'into a country of uncontaminated delight and loveliness and freedom, not unknown, but more or less forgotten. And fresh and sweet are its airs and scenes, its dreams and solemn absurdities, its perennial nonsense and enthusiasms . . .'—*Cubwood* never received the attention it deserved, and must now be long out of print. And as the world of childhood never dates itself out of all meaning and force, somebody, perhaps Sir Allen Lane, ought to re-issue *Cubwood*.

It must have been later in the autumn of 1922, for the weather had broken, that Davison and I set out one Sunday for a long walk, somewhere Richmond way. We returned to eat dinner in one of our greasy and smelly little restaurants, and then remembered we had been invited to a party that night at Queen's Gate given by Robert and Sylvia Lynd, soon to be among my closest friends. We were wearing tweeds and muddy walking shoes, but as it was Sunday night, we imagined, not unreasonably, that we were being asked to join a few of our literary elders for an informal drink. So off we went to Queen's Gate, to discover, when it was too late to retire, that in the Lynds' large drawing-room was most of literary London in full evening dress. Among the

C.T.L.—E

guests, seeming in our fancy to pull themselves away from us a little, were fabulous beings like Shaw and Wells and Bennett, no longer caricatures but living breathing men, chattering away in easily recognizable accents. This must have been the beginning, a sadly oafish entry, of much party-going that ran right through the 'twenties and 'thirties. As I have pointed out elsewhere, these large evening parties, superior in every way to the cocktail parties that gradually superseded them, had more than a social value. They made something like a literary society possible. They enabled young writers to meet, on easy convivial terms, their distinguished elders, who became men and women instead of being mere names, reputations, outlooks and styles. This encouraged a healthy feeling of continuity in letters. It helped to banish those peculiar and often morbid notions that young writers cherish in loneliness. The elderly and famous, now fellow guests in search of a drink and a sandwich, ceased to be legendary figures or monstrous ruins barring the way for the young. I count it another piece of luck that I came to London when such parties were still given, and youthful writers, however oafish and bumptious, were invited to them. Literary London would be better off, far more soundly based, if we returned to the habit of giving such parties, open to writers of all ages. If our grim economics prevent private persons from giving them, then publishers and editors, with solid expense accounts behind them, should fulfil the need. For if I do not know, as I should like to know, more than ten writers under 40, the fault is not mine: I am never invited where I might find

more of them. But in 1922 you could begin taking a
good look at your colleagues. There may have been
feuds among the shindies, but the atmosphere of authorship was neither sour nor desolate.

We youngsters, having neither the money nor the
space, were of course always guests and never hosts at
those large full-dress affairs. But we gave and received
a lot of hospitality of our own modest kind. Food,
drink and service were still comparatively cheap. In
Soho, for which I soon left the Fulham and King's
Roads, you could buy a dinner for two shillings, and for
ten shillings you could add a bottle of wine, a brandy or
two, a cigar with your coffee. My own favourite place,
discovered a little later, was the one-roomed *Escargot*
in Greek Street, not to be confused with the more
ambitious restaurant, run by the same family, on the
opposite side of the street. There were only about four
tables in the original restaurant, which might have been
transported, proprietor and all, from any French small
town. It was no use hurrying in there for a theatre
dinner, for they did not keep a number of cooked dishes
ready to be warmed up for the table; your order was
shouted by the proprietor, usually with a word of com-
mendation for your choice, down the shaft into the
kitchen below; and it was usually about two hours or so
before you were asking for their black and bitter coffee.
The son opened a good place across the way, but my
heart remained with the father, who looked like a
French general of the old school.

I rarely patronized the better-known restaurants,
such as the *Eiffel Tower*, which served as meeting places

for painters and writers. Our haunt was the pub, just
one longish bar, in Poppins Court, underneath the
London Mercury offices. There, every week-day between twelve-thirty and two, was a gathering of wits
who produced the liveliest talk I ever remember hearing. Squire and Shanks and many of the regular contributors to the *London Mercury* would often be joined by
Lynd, James Bone, George Mair, Belloc, J. B. Morton,
Bohun Lynch and many another good talker. Other
places where we sometimes met were the *Rainbow* and
the wine vaults under Ludgate Circus. I have sometimes
thought that this overfondness for drink and good talk
from midday onwards was partly responsible for a
marked change—not, in my view, for the better—in
English literary criticism, values and fashions. Some of
these convivial souls, with others I have not named,
talked away the books they ought to have written, books
in which they could have displayed their love, knowledge, and understanding of literature, their ability to
relate it to life, books that would have been at once
urbane and generous yet sharply critical of any writing
that lacked either heart or mind. And it was about this
time, I feel, that the reading public was fatally divided
into high, low and middle brows, that writing began to
be assessed not in terms of its own qualities, which are
what the true critic should be concerned with, but in
terms of its possible audience, that writers whose books
began to sell (and I have yet to meet one who did not
want his books to sell) were denounced at once as char-
latans. More than thirty years have passed, the world
has been turned upside down, but we are still suffering

from this change of literary climate. There were too
many rounds, too much talk, in those pubs. But it was
fun at the time; and I suspect that our newest writers,
even though not disdaining pubs, could do with a few
sessions of such talk.

Good theatre seats were comparatively dear then,
just as they are comparatively cheap now, so if we
could not find somebody, a dramatic critic or friendly
editor, to give us complimentary tickets, we went in the
pit or gallery. I remember paying about ninepence or so
at the old Alhambra to see the most astonishing galaxy
of prima ballerinas that ever blazed on one stage. And
the Lyric, Hammersmith, was cheap enough, and there
Nigel Playfair's production of *The Beggar's Opera* was
running. We knew every word and note of it, used to
roar them out round the piano, but still returned, time
after time, to the Lyric. It seemed to me then—and after
a quarter of a century of work in the Theatre, I am not
prepared to change my mind—an enchanting production, the best in its kind we have ever had in this
country, never beaten by later attempts to get away
from Playfair's style, Lovat Fraser's decor, Frederick
Austin's modest but rather luscious arrangement of the
music. On the other hand, although I saw the production, I was never an enthusiastic admirer of the other
long run, *The Immortal Hour*, at another old theatre
brought out of shabbiness and neglect, the Regent, near
King's Cross. But if you wanted perfection of a very
different theatrical style, extreme naturalism, there
were the productions of Galsworthy's plays by Basil
Dean at the St Martin's, where so many good actors

learnt their trade. You might dislike this kind of play, this method of production, yet could not deny Dean the triumph of his formidable qualities, which we are beginning to miss in the Theatre. There was also some good new work being done up at the Everyman Theatre, Hampstead, by Norman Macdermott. And Gerald du Maurier, who as actor-manager had every virtue except the courage necessary for experiment, was still at Wyndham's. I was told not long ago, by way of a rebuke, that our London post-war Theatre might no longer be creative but that it has reached greatness in its interpretation; but it seems to me—and I speak of one of my own trades—that outside Shakespeare both the production and acting in the 'twenties were generally superior to ours. But then the economics of the Theatre were much sounder. It had hardly begun to have colossal rivals that drew on its talent without making any adequate return for their loans and raids.

During the last few years the intimate revue, which I have always preferred to musical comedy, has been revived with considerable success, and I fancy it offers us more genuine satire and wit than it did thirty years ago. But I do not think it is mere age that makes me believe the original *Nine O'Clock Revue* at the Little and the early Charlot revues were much better, filled with richer talent, bigger personalities, funnier sketches more artful tunes. And what is certain is that the music-hall of today is nothing but the ghost of what it was in the early 'twenties in London. It had already passed its peak even then, but some of the ripe old turns were still with us. You could look in at the Coliseum, as I often did on a winter afternoon, and see Little Tich and Harry Tate, and there were still some glorious drolls at the Holborn Empire (a sad loss; it had a fine thick atmosphere of its own), the Victoria Palace, and the rest. There were no microphones and nobody needed them. There were no stars who had arrived by way of amusing farmers' wives and invalids on the radio. There were no reputations that had been created by American gramophone records for teenagers. The men and women who topped the bills had spent years getting there, learning how to perfect their acts and to handle their audiences. Of course there was plenty of vulgar rubbish, but all but the very worst of it had at least some zest and vitality. And the audiences, which laughed at jokes and did not solemnly applaud them as BBC audiences do now, were an essential part of the show; they too had vitality, and were still close to the Cockneys who helped to create, a generation earlier, the English music-hall of the great period, the folk art out of which, among other things, came the slapstick of the silent films, especially those of Chaplin.

I was never out of London very long throughout the 'twenties, and probably would never have left it at all if I had not had a young family, for I soon came to feel an affection for the sprawling monster. Even its shocking extremes of wealth and poverty I disliked more in theory than in actuality. I was fond of wandering about in it and taking buses and trams to its remote suburbs, and must have written scores of essays—I wrote at least one essay a week for many years—that had a London background, as well as one long novel, *Angel Pavement*.

Its life then had many blots that have now been sponged
out. There is now far less truly appalling misery. But
most other changes have been for the worse. There is
now far more cheap spivvery, even in the West End.
The kind of subhuman faces you see in the neon lighting
of Coventry Street any night now, passing like an un-
ending parade of the seven deadly sins, I do not remember seeing when I was first in London. Many of the best
little old shops, eating houses, pubs, seem to have
vanished, and in their places are shoddy establishments
that look like Broadway rejects. London in fact has been
Americanized, and not by what is best but by what is
worst in America, by over-advertised soft drinks and
not by unadvertised old bourbon, by snack bars and
cafeterias and not by sea-food restaurants and steak
houses, by boogie-woogies and not by the Boston Sym-
phony. And because of the intolerable strain of contemporary metropolitan living, the growing defeat of human
zest and sympathy by the mere mechanics of existence,
London, like New York and Paris, is rapidly becoming
a bad-tempered city, filled with the sour smell of that
defeat.

No doubt if I were arriving again as a young man,
scurrying round not only to make a living, to establish
myself, but also to explore and to savour this vast
oyster-bed of a capital, I would see a different London,
one perhaps far closer to the city I began to discover in
the autumn of 1922. I believe, as I never for an hour
ceased to believe then, that I could make my way in it.
But I am not sorry that I am not having my try now. I
had a harder time, for private and tragic reasons, than I

have suggested here, worked all day and half the night for a long unhappy period, with one burden piled on another; but even so, given my profession, I fancy I chose the right time both to be born and to arrive in London. Yes, I had the luck.

Elizabeth Bowen

ALL through my childhood, London had a fictitious existence for me. It loomed darkly somewhere at the other side of the water; I thought of it (when at all) as an entity, at once magnetic and dangerous. It was, from all I heard, a city into which no one ventured alone, and which was to be entered only after preparation and wary forethought. It stood for the adult, and so much so that there should be children in London seemed unimaginable—in fact that there should be people of any kind was only a secondary idea: I pictured the thing as a mass of building, a somehow impious extreme of bulk and height in whose interstices was fog. I first crossed the city when I first crossed the sea, when I was 4: it must have been winter, we arrived after dark and were driven as hurriedly as possible from Euston to some other terminus in a cab. The street lamps, seeming dimmer than Dublin's, showed us to be in the continuous bottom of a chasm, among movement conveying a sense of trouble, and which one suspected rather than saw. My mother for a minute put down a window, saying, as though in extenuation, 'London has a smell of its own.' But this, like all else given off, was non-human.

I do not know when, at what later date, I came to

know that the sun shone there—that is to say, there also—or when I took in that this, like some planet, also must be taken to be inhabited. If I had been an American child instead of an Anglo-Irish one, it is possible that London, from being farther in the distance, would have been more clear-cut as an idea: I should have had some rational notion of it, instead of being infested by it imaginatively. As it was, it was like a hand too near my eyes. Nobody ever told me about London, or explained to me what or why it was—I was assumed, I suppose, to have been born knowing. This may have come from the Anglo-Irish ambivalence as to all things English, a blend of impatience and evasiveness, a reluctance to be pinned down to a relationship— one which, all the same, nobody could have conceived of life without. So for what seems a long time London remained partly a not quite convincing fiction, partly a symbol of ambiguity, partly an overcast physical fact. Even when my mother and I went to live in the South of England we almost never took the train to the capital. Though we knew *of* quite a number of people who lived in London, we visited only one or another aunt or my mother's godmother, to whom we glued ourselves onward from Charing Cross. My mother knew she would lose her way. For my part, each time I looked for London it had jiggled itself into a different pattern. Nothing like a picture was to be formed.

The picture, when it did form, came out of books— as I could not read easily till I was over 7, and did not begin to read novels till I was 10, it came late. It was composite, geographically wrong and intensely vivid, pieced together out of Dickens, E. F. Benson, E. Nesbit, Galsworthy, Conan Doyle and of course Compton Mackenzie. I also read many Edwardian novels in which Park Lane featured, and for some reason I saw this overhanging the Thames (really more like Riverside Drive overhanging the Hudson in New York). This envisaged London gained on me something of the obsessive hold of a daydream; it invested itself with a sensuous reality—sounds, smells, motes of physical atmosphere—so powerful as to have been equalled since by almost no experience of so-called reality. Even the weather was dramatic: fogs impenetrable, summers Mediterranean, sunsets lurid and nights gothic with pitchblack shadows. And I endowed London with extremes of fashion and wealth, alongside which lay sinister squalor. Fancy was slow to encompass the middle reaches. This romanticist's London I have never extirpated from my heart—and, like a renewed vision it does now and then, even now, reappear. Probably the magic of a city, as of a person, resides in its incapacity to be known, and the necessity therefore that it should be imagined.

Imaginative writing, fiction, was my only data for London till I was nearly 20. Bayswater was the first region to project into my personal life, for here lived two or three of my friends at boarding-school, whom I used to visit on my way across London at the beginnings or ends of term. Theirs were the first doors I ever saw opening upon interiors—which themselves never seemed quite credible, or at any rate wholly everyday. Leaving my friends behind, I realized that their existences while apart from me were almost literally a closed book, and went back to books capable of being opened —that is, actual ones. Nothing made full sense to me that was not in print. Life seemed to promise to be intolerable without full sense, authoritative imaginative knowledge. Feeling what a book could do, and what indeed only a book *could* do, made me wish to write: I conceived of nothing else as worth doing. At the same time, what attributes were required? Could one be a writer and not a demigod? I became most anxious to be in the presence of one or two, not so much I think out of curiosity as in the hope that virtue proceeded from them. Oh to be at least in the outer precincts, whatever came of it.

In these days I cannot believe it possible that anybody should live to the age of 19 without having encountered an author. At Folkestone a disastrous cold in the head had prevented my setting eyes on Baroness Orczy; E. V. Lucas's daughter was at my school, but when he came there I was never around. My County Cork home was eighty-five miles away from Edith Somerville's, but that was a distance, before motor cars. At last, near Limerick, at my father's wedding to my stepmother I met her magnificent brother, Stephen Gwynn—talk with him confirmed me in my idea: generally, authors lived in London. So back I went, this time with intention. As a sort of disguise, I worked at the LCC School of Art in Southampton Row, near which trams rushed up out of the earth. My Earls Court lodgings had the merit of being round the corner from Lilley Road, mentioned in *Sinister Street*. When I moved in,

theatrical autumn sunshine bathed this first part of
London I was on domestic terms with, and thin blonde
leaves drifted through the air. . . . The year after, I
changed my locale, going to live with a great-aunt in
Queen Anne's Gate. My existence there, beautiful as it
was, seemed to be missing in one dimension—unac-
countably, I had not yet found Westminster in a story.
It was too bad that Virginia Woolf had not by then
written *Mrs. Dalloway.*

The winters of 1919, '20 and '22 run together: I
cannot always remember which was which. (1921, I
was in Italy.) The London of then—I mean, the London I sought—could not have been kinder to that most
awkward of creatures, a literary aspirant. Looking back,
I fancy that there were, then, more aspirants, fewer
very young authors. Not one of the great I met asked
me why I was not at a university, as no doubt I should
have been. At Oxford or Cambridge, I expect I should
have talked about ideas; in London I was careful to
keep my mouth shut, listening to talkers like a spy.
Apart from schoolfriends I met again, I had not much
interest in my contemporaries—I could only think about
The Elect. My idea of contemporary artists was a sacer-
dotal one. I had read their work not only with absorp-
tion but a kind of piety; everything but their appearances
was known to me. (The putting of authors' photographs
on book-jackets was not then, for better or worse, in
practice.) I could not wait to be where they moved and
spoke.

The big orange *London Mercury* was the dominating
magazine. The Poetry Bookshop was a *foyer:* upstairs,

after dark, in a barn-like room, I listened to Ezra Pound
reading aloud what was hypnotically unintelligible to
me by the light of one candle. The beginning of my life
as the greater part of it has been since was when I was
asked to tea to meet Rose Macaulay at the University
Women's Club: this I owed to her friend, my head-
mistress, Olive Willis. In youth, and I suppose always,
it is kindness with a touch of imaginative genius that
one rates most highly: this I had from Rose. She lit up
a confidence I had never had: having written stories, I
showed them to her. With her I met Naomi Royde-
Smith, then editing *The Saturday Westminster*: it was in
those pages that a story of mine first appeared in print.
But something more: there were Naomi's and Rose's
memorable evening parties—Thursdays, I think. I went,
supported by Mary Hope Allen. Inconceivably, I found
myself in the same room as Edith Sitwell, Walter de la
Mare, Aldous Huxley; and I know there were others. I
remember almost unearthly electric light broken on
brocade-angular folds of one poet's dress, and her bene-
volence (she was talking about something lost under a
sofa) and the graven face and shining cavern eyes of the
other. Of Aldous Huxley I was most nearly frightened,
through no fault of his. But alas these images, and so
many since, cast themselves on the screen as a silent
film: I have a wonderful visual memory but a poor ver-
bal one. I recall little or anything that has been at any
time *said*—the sense and atmosphere of a conversation,
yes, but the words no. And all things considered, this is
a tragedy.

I suppose that literary London then was, as it is now,

multi-cellular. That was not a thing a young provincial was likely to realize. Many of the older writers I know now, it could have been possible to meet them. In one or two cases, D. H. Lawrence, Katherine Mansfield, it was then or never: I never did meet them—but then, I hardly knew them till they were dead. My relations with London were discontinuous: for twelve years after I married I did not live there. I went to London, off and on, for a day or two at a time: strictly I think that these recollections should be called 'Going [not Coming] to London'. It was a matter of sporadic approaches, different and shifting centres of interest. I lived through the nineteen-twenties without being aware of or taking part in them: they were a placid decade of my own existence. I recall successions of parties, each of which may have stood for a further phase or a change of focus. New planets were appearing in the sky. I recall with gratitude John Strachey's 1924 literary-editorship of *The Spectator*. Cyril Connolly, whose first novel to review for *The New Statesman* had been the first novel I had written, I met at the house of Miss Ethel Sands: later, there were Cyril's and Jean's deeply enjoyable parties in the King's Road. I did not know Virginia Woolf or T. S. Eliot till I met them both at Lady Ottoline Morrell's, in Gower Street, in the early 'thirties. . . . I can give the sensations of my protracted London half-life better than I can give the facts: the scrappiness and subjective vagueness of this record are inherent in its attempt at truth. I *came* to London, with any finality, only when we came to live there, in 1935, in Regent's Park—and by then first impressions were over. The

attraction of Regent's Park, the immediate sense that
this place was habitable, were due to its seeming something out of (or in) a book. And throughout seventeen
years, it did never wholly emerge from art. It was much
as I had fancied London would be.

Geoffrey Grigson

'THE fool,' said a short, ruby-cheeked, unmarried, elderly, black-bead-eyed cousin, encountered by the laurels at a bend in the drive, 'whistled as he went for want of thought.' She had brought up her younger brothers and sisters; and I was going to London— whistling, no doubt as I went, as at the time, in circumstances which were untidy and which she did not approve.

To begin with, I should have gone already, my unconferred altogether useless B.A. (English Language and Literature) wrapped around me; but I should have gone to Norwich, not to London; I should have been earning—was the word—already earning, in a mustard factory, having planted myself in a milieu altogether disturbing and strange, under a film of yellow dust. I had balked at the last moment; and now, at the next moment, was going to London, without a job. Was I 'burning to write'? Did I feel a yeast, or yeastful lumps, of words inside me? Nothing so clear, nothing so compelling. London was a vocable, not a place, not exactly a goal; two hundred and fifty miles away, this vocable stood for the end of adolescence, it stood for *doing*; at least, it stood for *beginning*, for *being in*, though exactly in what? Not in Burma, or India, or Norwich, or in

82

business. At any rate, it stood broadly and abstractedly
for the centre and for possibility, by writing.

But it was, after all, still six months before I came
among the capital stenches of possibility; for a while,
funking the unfamiliar a second time (as I had funked
the unfamiliarity of Norwich and mustard, and a race of
lean men I had met, so far, only once, and only for a
brief while in an office and across the table of a board-
room), I now sidled back into circumstances I knew. I
went, not to London, but to a school, of a kind, where I
taught boys, of a kind; so adding another term to the
terms of childhood, merely changing positions from
convict to keeper, keepers on their days off being at any
rate free to take the bus from Tonbridge into Tun-
bridge Wells, where bookshops and talk about books
to a bookshop proprietor with a black patch over one
eye or eye-socket could be deserted quickly for a girl,
who might, after all, consent to tea in the Pantiles, or
consent to talk among the hawthorns between the out-
croppings of stone, or go into the enclosing dark of a
cinema.

This was 1928 and 1929. I think bookishness was
then more in vogue. When I now read Mr Oliver
Edwards in *The Times*, the camphor-ball smell takes me
back to the period which was still undelivered from
Hazlitt, E. V. Lucas and G. K. Chesterton (though
Chesterton was already Wyndham Lewis's 'fierce, foam-
ing toby jug'); and when I reached London at last, and
at last was absorbed, stationed, a little rooted even,
inside the vocable, it was to a middle bookishness in
the seats of power that I went on paying, at first, my

mental subscription. Bookishness made much at that time of a poet named Humbert Wolfe. At Oxford I had borrowed Eliot's poems, from the Union Library; I had bought Humbert Wolfe's, from Thornton's; and here, in the vocable, this Humbert Wolfe existed. He read poems in a long upper chamber above the publishing office of Ernest Benn. I attended, obscurely. From a corner I observed daffodils on the table, the clasped hands of the poet, other poets, and rapt ladies. I was allowed, and encouraged myself, too, to call upon Jack Squire (as one heard him referred to), in an office full of bookish dismay and sentimental untidiness at what I should call, in a Twenties terminology, the E. V. Lucas end of Fleet Street; and I do not blame this editor who looked so like an editor in the part of an editor, for making so little of a caller so tentative, so much without *nous* that he did not even ask, or dare to ask, for books to review. I proclaimed no juvenile faith—I had none—for which Squire should have been thankful. I told him, I think, vaguely and with no flow of syllables that I thought I might find, and perhaps he could tell me how to find, a job—was not this Fleet Street?—on a newspaper. He was polite in his excusable boredom, he lifted his head from his waistcoat, unreviewed and I suppose unsaleable books and bulging folders in that hutch seeming likely to topple on him and bury him prematurely, and turning on me a mask histrionically and professionally *blunt*, perhaps modelled on the face of Sir Joshua Reynolds, who came like himself from Plymouth, he asked, 'Are you interested—in *politics?*'

Oafish altogether at my own futility, I told him I

was not; which seemed to him (H'm. A pity) to decide
me and the matter. He picked up his pen. I hesitated.
This might have been the moment to speak of poems,
aspirations, and then book reviews—had I ever
reviewed a book. I did not mention poems to him, I did
not fumble and offer him poems, I did not say that I
wrote poems. I had not the nerve—for which again he
should have been grateful. He wagged his pen above
paper, and I left, stumbling over books, and glad of
sunshine outside on a building I did not know was the
Law Courts.

Why should I have thought that 'coming to London'
entailed coming here to this office of the *London Mercury?* Wasn't there also, and had I not encountered it at
Oxford, a *New Criterion* with its covers bright lemon
and red instead of drably orange like the covers of the
Mercury, and with T. S. Eliot for editor? Wasn't there
also a particular world of writers—no, at this time, I
did not know of differing worlds of writers—weren't
there also a number of individual writers I had seen and
listened to, as an undergraduate? Didn't Robert Graves
exist, and sharp little Laura Riding? And silvery Mrs
Woolf? And goggle-hidden Aldous Huxley? And, though
I had neither seen him nor heard him, did not there also
exist a D. H. Lawrence, who in a poem, in an anthology
I had been given, published by the Poetry Bookshop,
had written about a girl whose breasts swayed like full-
blown Gloire de Dijon roses (such roses, in fact, as
swayed above my mother's drawing-room window)?

These were remote. They were still remote, at least, if
one was young and if one had been lapped in bookishness,

which is a pimping and so approachable activity. I
might, I suppose, have asked myself where certain poets
of Oxford were now to be found (who were still finding
themselves)—Louis MacNeice, who had stalked lanes
around Merton blackavisiedly in a cloak, knowing, elegant, writing of 'that never-satisfied old maid, the sea',
who 'Rehangs her white lace curtains ceaselessly', who
in later times was to own a borzoi which curled around
furniture in Keats Grove, Clere Parsons, elegant and
fair, Thomas Driberg, knowing and disdainful, Wystan
Hugh Auden, who had taken a third in English but had
found the blood of Grendel luminous along the moor?
But these were not established, they wrote poems—had
written poems—but in a way (Hardy was still alive)
they were not 'poets' yet. They had another remote-
ness, of a not quite real undergraduate atmosphere one
had left. In the haze, the incomer into London sees at all
clearly at first only those who are collected works or
have been established publicly. The influence still on
him, in spite of the university, of the reading of elder
brothers (an elder brother of mine read the *London
Mercury* and had written poems which were a mixture
of *Grongar Hill* and John Drinkwater), and of families,
of schools, and school libraries and particular masters,
the infant in London does not detect groupings and
distinctions all at once. Authors are wonderful; for a
little while most of them are archangels and all archangels are white (and most, or the most obvious, archangels then were bookish ones). The incomer cannot
tell all at once who has borrowed his wing-feathers,
who is hired, who is not for sale, who is smudged, whose

consciousness is pure; he must know a little more of himself before he can know enough of the others. Then, indeed, comes—or may come—that illumination, that extraordinary maturity of recognition at least, in the midst of immaturity, that certainty about which are the few advancing tendrils of pure consciousness in one's time. One is—or may be—released into an apprehension which does not last perhaps for a great while, since most of us tend to be reabsorbed into false or impure consciousness. It is as if we were born in a tunnel; we break out for a while, our being emerges like a train into sunshine along the edge of a sea (I think of the Dawlish tunnels in the anchovy-sauce-coloured rocks, which I had passed through so often as a child) and then the tunnel encloses us once more, the shafts of light becoming fewer, the darkness and self-righteousness of a social conceit becoming more palpable; or we may be those who are always in the tunnel, permeated all our lives by the common acceptable darkness, mistaking bats always for angels.

Humbert Wolfe clasping his hands by the fresh daffodillies, his hair elongated to a pad above the back of his neck, Jack Squire hunched and hutched and blunt among dead books as among the fossilized ordure of hyenas in a cave—these were accessible; and such accessibility was quickly educative. It soon distinguished Others, soon created a recognition of *The Others*, who were not accessible, happening to live in a wood beyond the edge of the world, in which they were guarded by an electric sanctity of the real thing. Humbert Wolfe I could see; a cut above him or the coprolite cave of the *London*

Mercury, I could see, indeed visit, indeed talk to, dark
Harold Monro in his Poetry Bookshop across from the
British Museum, and buy books from him ('waste all
that money on Doughty,' said Monro, putting the volumes
of *The Dawn in Britain* back on a high shelf, and making
me, with his habitual frown of impatience, buy *Grace
after Meat* by John Crowe Ransom, introduced by Robert
Graves, at a cost of 4s 6d instead of 35s or so). Yet to
have conversed with, for example, D. H. Lawrence at
that time would have seemed to me no less presumptu-
ous than to have plucked a red hair out of his beard.

Fleet Street may seem an odd road to take towards
the recognition of pure consciousness. Contraries, though,
reveal each other. I had tried also the other end of Fleet
Street, and with a different trepidation had been carried
upwards in a shaky lift, inside the office of *The Times*, to
a bare, brisk room occupied by Robin Barrington-Ward,
at that time an assistant editor, and not editor. For me,
had I quite realized it, this was a rare and daring plunge
into what Henry Fairlie quite correctly names the Establishment. But Barrington-Ward came from the parish
which across a wild valley had adjoined my own in
Cornwall, child of a neighbouring parsonage, though he
had been long weaned of such provinciality by Oxford,
by the presidency of the Union and by touching the
hems of the morning-coats of power and importance. I
left his important, sharp presence (looking up from his
bare corner, he resembled a well-dressed, neatly-beaked,
bald-browed finch in an engraving after Grandville)
with advice which would have been excellent if I had
not, hazily, forgotten most of it before I reached the lift

again—excellent, that is to say, had I also been of suitable stuff to graduate, at last, with the hand of Lionel Curtis on my head, pin-striped at some very future date, to the staff of *The Times*, Meanwhile, I had nothing, he said, to offer to a London paper, yet; I must try the Provinces, first. That much I remembered, but I was in London, I had no intention of getting out of London.

In the lift was a very junior member of this staff of *The Times* whom I had known, or just known, as an undergraduate; and before the lift reached the ground he had given me far better advice, which it was not difficult at all to remember. Age speaking to like age, he had given me a name, a number to ring at once, and an address to go to in Fleet Street, for bread-and-butter undeferred.

That was that. I was among journalists; there were journalists—two, at any rate—who talked about Wyndham Lewis and Newman's *Apologia*, about theology, destiny and *Time and Western Man*, while enduring my silence at the same Fleet Street table. But did I meet archangelic authors? Not in Fleet Street. What writers of any kind had I *talked* to—not merely read, or seen, or looked at sideways, or as it were overheard? Once, but that was long ago, the novelist May Sinclair, who was a cousin or connexion of my mother's; a meeting which did not count, since through lunch she was an emancipated woman who was in the know, scoring off a parson's wife who was in the vicarage. Once, eating a supper, alone, of course, at the Café Royal (I knew about the Café Royal) before I had rooted myself in London, I had been spoken to by Edgar Wallace. That also did not count; he warned me that a wise man did not show the pound notes in his pocket book, as I had shown them paying the bill, and then conducted me round some odd smoky corners of the purlieus of Leicester Square, before I took a taxi to Paddington for a midnight train back to Cornwall, my home and my bookishness.

It happened that the *Yorkshire Post*, on which, in its London office in Fleet Street, I had now gained my undeferred bread-and-butter, possessed an author of its own—Alice Herbert, forgotten now, a novelist who then wrote for the paper a weekly review of novels. She was quick, kind, sentimental, full of spirit, the mother of Ivy Low and so the mother-in-law of Litvinov. Humbert Wolfe's pad of greasy poetical hair had begun to push me from bookishness; so, in another way, I was pushed from it by tea once a week with Alice Herbert, below the palms of the Aldwych Hotel, casting a half-shadow of *belles lettres* and a recollection of literary sex which she enjoyed, and in which she spoke low, huskily, and intensely. Under her hair dyed as black as a fountain-pen, with eyes to match, old Alice Herbert was not herself an archangel, exactly; she was no Collected Works, but had graduated downwards from novels to novel reviewing for the *Observer*, and so, downwards again, to the *Yorkshire Post*. Her son-in-law was at any rate a notable Prince of Darkness, and she was acquainted with many older writers—with Bennett, who still walked under a jaunty quiff on the London pavements, for example, and Wells. And not in the Aldwych but in her little upstairs flat in Brooke Green she introduced

me to my first snowy, pinnacled, indubitable archangel
—to T. S. Eliot. I admit that on that occasion, on that
afternoon in early summer, he never flew down over
the green banks of tree foliage above the London street,
never entered by the window, never folded his long
angelic, majestic wings before folding leg over leg as
he began to drink tea; he arrived—greatest archangel
of them all to me by that time—in an Austin Seven (I
watched him from the window) when Austin Sevens
were each like a deep sardine tin; he came with a small
pointed English Mrs Eliot, and with an active, yappy,
up and down little dog, which was perpetually off the
archangel's lap and on it again. 'Why?' said small Mrs
Eliot, tartly and sharply, to statements passed unchal-
lengingly across the sandwiches. This archangel, this
(to the Squirearchy) giant Reprobus of Letters who was
to be converted into tame, acceptable and accepted St
Christopher, put his hands together and refolded leg
equivocally over leg and explained with gentleness; he
was gentle also to the innocent statements, which were
neither sparkling nor wise.

I was to owe more to the friendship and encourage-
ment of the Ogre of Letters, Wyndham Lewis, that
splendid Polypheme—all eye, intelligence and energy—
of modern literature, than to this gentler equivocal
giant; but that was later, after I had been bringing out
New Verse for a time.

Retrospectively I now recognize in myself a special
loneliness as I came into the play of London. If you
cannot bring yourself to assault the company of any of
the archangels of your admiration, and if the hirelings

and self-deluded or art-deluded depress you, then you
have to live in a special loneliness until the finding of
what you are and your work and activities and your
luck attract the special company you need. Several years
later, when my friend Hugh Ross Williamson and I
squeezed out of an evening's talk in the winter in Keat's
Grove the project and plan of *New Verse*, I hardly believed (still believing in archangels) that certain creatures of eminence, Eliot, Read and I. A. Richards, for
example, would stoop to reply, as they did, with interest, to letters asking them for the blessing of contribu-
tions to the first number of a small magazine with an
obscure editor. All these other archangels or sub-angels
stood for, was then less entrenched. It was worth doing
anything to assault daffydowndillyism or the false standards of a Literary Establishment which I have not
mentioned and which could now do, as much as the
other, allied, surviving Establishment, with an historical
analysis. What had Coleridge who knew Fleet Street
and the rest of London writing, to say to a young
American? That he could, but wouldn't, introduce him
to most of the authors of London; he would not have
his young American corrupted; he told him seriously
that 'he did not know so entirely worthless and despic-
able a set of men as the authors by profession in London.'
Fair enough for that time, for the late 'twenties, for the
'thirties, for now, I daresay; but I am not so sure about
the wisdom of Coleridge's refusal: the few angels are
to be recognized all the more firmly, then appreciated
all the more finely, if you are able to contrast them, at
first hand, with the diversity of hell-hounds.

About not being in London, Wyndham Lewis remarked to me that he, at any rate, as an author had
'never found it safe to live more than ten minutes from
Notting Hill Gate'. But coming and staying are different
affairs; and it was my experience that special, self-
guarding loneliness needs an ordinary company, and
also needs around it for a while, at least, all the hell-
hounds, all the self-elected, all the hirelings of London,
with all of the one city's more positively rousing and
tempering elements. For how can one's special loneliness ripen at all without the one great grey Babylon of
meanings and revelations which 'easily becomes, on its
face, a garden bristling with an immense illustrative
flora', without the one place where whores fight by the
Lex Garage, and seedy reviewers still sell their review
books, and journalists grow old and believe their own
lies, and publishers hop like fat crows after offal; among
which offal all the same, the *Bacchus* and *Ariadne* burns
and sparkles in Trafalgar Square, 'a thing,' as Henry
James once said in his own early days in London, 'to go
barefoot to see'?

John Middleton Murry

THERE are many Londons. Certainly, at a given moment in my life, I 'came to London'. But I had known three Londons before that one. I was born in London, in a shabby street off the Old Kent Road. Thence, as my father climbed his way out of the proletariat of the early 'nineties, we moved first to Peckham and then to East Dulwich. The whole movement was typical of the times. For my father had come to London in the aboriginal sense of the phrase. He came to it out of Kent, and he pitched his tent as near as possible to the road by which he came. The Old Kent Road for him was the road back into Kent: it secured his line of communication. In case of defeat, he could retire along it. To me the Old Kent Road brought no such assurance. It was only a name for a terrifying highway that went on and on for ever. I scuttled across it, like a little cat, neither so quick nor so sure-footed.

To move away from it, if only to Peckham and East Dulwich, meant that my father had gained a foothold. He had managed to get into the old War Office, as what was then called a 'writer', and has since become a type-writer: for he simply copied fair, in his beautiful and fluent script, the tangled drafts of letters handed down to him by the superior beings above. I was told about these magnificos. They arrived at ten o'clock, in hansom cabs when it was wet; they went to lunch at their clubs at one, and returned at three. They drafted more letter till half-past four, and then they departed. One or two of them stayed during lunch time, in case war broke out in the interval; and they had elegant meals brought to them in their rooms. One of these had the gracious habit of offering my father a glass of claret when he went to collect the drafted letters. I saw this splendid being once. My father had told him that I was standing for a scholarship for Christ's Hospital; then that I had got one. Whereupon Mr S. had asked to see me, because he was an Old Blue. Considering how shocked he must have been to know that a Board School boy had been thrust upon the Religious, Royal and Ancient Foundation to which he had belonged, it speaks much for his kindness that he congratulated me as I stood petrified with shyness, and gave me a golden sovereign, which he clicked out of a sovereign purse.

That, I felt, was one of the mysterious and magnificent things that happened 'in London'. For London was not where I lived. It began across Waterloo Bridge, whither I sometimes penetrated to meet my father on his return from the office. He, every day, walked through Champion Hill down the long and beautiful Camberwell Grove (where, he told me, the great Joseph Chamberlain used to live) to Camberwell Green, where he took a penny horse-tram to the bridge: then he walked over the bridge to Whitehall. This long walk, which I also took when I met him, set London at the end of a pilgrimage, a remote and bewildering city, over the hills and far away.

But it was of yet another London that I became a denizen when, at Queen Victoria's death, I entered the Bluecoat School in Newgate Street. This was the City. I now felt myself to be a minuscule subject of the Lord Mayor, to whom I bowed as a candle-boy at the Lenten Supper, holding two flower-begirt candlesticks in either hand. But the City he governed was a patchwork to me. The Old Bailey, over the way, was an impressive part of it; and so was the City Marshal, who attended the Lord Mayor, in a bright scarlet uniform and a plumed hat like the Duke of Wellington's. So was St Paul's; and so were the Companies, the incredible dessert of whose gargantuan feasts some of us were permitted to share, by an odd prescriptive right. And so, above all, was the Tower of London, where bluecoats and yellow stockings were admitted free.

Then came the exodus. Christ's Hospital parted from the City for ever. The dames of the wards gave way to the masters of houses. The old Tudor divisions—the Writing School, the Grammar School, the Mathematical School—were swept away. The asceticism of unheated wards and rugby football on asphalte vanished. And from the rural distance of Horsham, the three Londons blended into one like a dissolving view in a magic-lantern show, because I had ceased to belong to any part of it. For my father, too, had gone rural, and rented a little red-brick cottage in Ewell, which was still recognizably a village, fifty-five years ago.

Having got out of London, I became scared of it, as I

was not before. Perhaps because I was becoming scared of most things. Even when, to my astonishment, I had won a classical scholarship to Oxford, nothing would induce me to go up the easy way through London. I sidled into Oxford and out of it by a devious route through Guildford and Reading, rather than face two London termini, and the piracy of a connecting cab.

I was all at sea. Even though Christ's Hospital had licked me into the semblance of a gentleman, and generously provided me with two exhibitions so that I was not very poor, I felt an imposter. I did not belong anywhere. I was ashamed of my uncultured home; and it shames me even now to write that I was. Yet I seemed to be totally devoid of ambition. I made quite a few good friends at Oxford, but I would have run to the ends of the earth rather than let them know that I had been a Board School boy. I was nothing but a bundle of antennae, feeling out for a new social persona. The idea of having to choose a career, and to make my living in the world, induced a kind of mental paralysis.

I used to spend my vacations in a remote Cotswold farmhouse, where the farmer and his wife made much of me. In that unlikely place I met a young officer in the French submarine service, called Maurice Larrouy, who had come there to learn English. He told me he was also a novelist, and presented me with a strange novel about the racial migrations in the Asian deserts. His pen-name was René Milan, and he afterwards wrote a minor masterpiece: *L'Odysée d'un Transport Torpillé*. He was ruthless in questioning me, and dragged out of me the

C.T.L.—G

confession that I dreamed of being a literary critic:
which was more a desperate reaction to the inquisition
of his positive mind than any formed desire of my own.
C'est bon! he declared, as though my velleity was an
entirely rational resolve to enter a very respectable profession, as literary criticism was and is in France. Having settled that, he set himself to organize my immediate future. I must go to Paris, because that was the
metropolis of criticism. And straightway he wrote off to
a shipmate of his to find me a cheap room near the Sorbonne. I had the feeling that I was *engagé:* much more
fearful than exultant.

Among the chief of my Oxford friends at this time
were Michael Sadleir and Joyce Cary. Michael introduced me to the French symbolists, with whom I duti-
fully struggled: also to the drawings of Augustus John,
of which his father had a notable collection. Joyce Cary
was one of a group of Trinity men, whom I found very
attractive. They were a little older than the average
undergraduate. Some of them had come on from Scottish
universities, while Joyce had put in a year at an art
school. Something had intervened for them between the
public school and the university, which made the difference. They were neither overgrown sixth-form boys,
like me, nor pass-men up for a good time. There was
nothing precious about them, yet their intellectual interests were various and widespread; and they judged
for themselves. To me they were vastly stimulating: I
can hardly have been that to them.

Joyce heartily approved my going to Paris, and said
that he would join me there. Nominally, I was going to

listen to Bergson at the Collège de France. I never went.
Before I knew where I was, I was entangled in all kinds
of new and exciting relations—with the Scots painters,
J. D. Fergusson and S. J. Peploe; with that connoisseur
of the Paris underworld, Francis Carco; with Arthur
Ransome, smoking his benign and ponderous calumet
in a corner of the Lilas; with a thrilling group of Esthonian poets and painters, who quietly told me horrible
stories of the suppression of their revolution in 1905 by
the Baltic barons. Perhaps most exciting of all were the
windows of the little shop of the *Cahiers de la Quinzaine*
in the Place de la Sorbonne, through which more than
once I gazed at Charles Pèguy himself packing up parcels
of his famous but ill-subscribed review. Thenceforward,
I could conceive nothing finer than to follow his example: to have a review like his, a little shop like his,
and to pack the parcels with my own hands.

Suddenly, Oxford seemed very far away. Wherever
my mental centre of gravity had been before (if anywhere) now it was somewhere quite different. All these
strangely various people belonged to an acknowledged
confraternity: they were artists. Art was their religion.
Whether it was Pèguy and his parcels, or Fergusson
stripped to the buff polishing the floor of his studio before starting work for the day, or Ourits, the Esthonian
painter, trying to make me understand that an oppressed
people's soul must necessarily find utterance through
art, it all converged to one end: that art was the *unum
necessarium*, in the service of which poverty was to be
expected and endured. And it was painfully obvious that
some of them had more than a fair share of it. The

draught was intoxicating. It took me months to gather myself together again.

What I should have liked to do was to go on living in Paris. But that was an impossible dream. I had no money. What I did was to join with Michael Sadleir in producing a strange hotch-potch of a quarterly magazine called *Rhythm* full of post-impressionist drawings and decorations, collected mainly by Fergusson. (To us, I believe, fell the unmerited honour of being the first to reproduce a Picasso in England.) Meanwhile, I pondered desperately how I could escape from Oxford, on which my small income wholly depended, and make a living by writing. In London it would have to be, if it was to be at all. And in London, surely, there must be some counterpart to that wonderful republic of art in Paris, if only one could find the entrance to it. So I acquired a typewriter, and sent verses to *The English Review*. They were returned with gloom-inducing expedition. *The New Age* printed an essay; *T.P's. Weekly* another, and even paid me four guineas. I ought to have felt encouraged, but I didn't. Joyce Cary, who now lived with me in rooms in Holywell, must have found me a depressing companion. But it would have taken more than that to disturb him in his sense of vocation. He covered the sitting-room floor with foolscap sheets of Caroline lyrics—about eight lines to the page; which was extravagant of paper but gave him a necessary feeling of elbow-room. For the same reason, I suppose, he did most of his writing on the floor, with an exceptionally blunt quill pen.

One day a story was sent to *Rhythm* by Katherine

Mansfield. It was a satirical fairy tale, of which the point eluded me; but it was obvious, even to me, that she was a writer. So I sent it back, and asked for another. It was *The Woman at the Store*. It does not rank with her finest work, which was to come later, but it was so remarkably different from anything that had come to *Rhythm* that I was wildly excited. Even Joyce, who was a little scornful of what was printed in *Rhythm*, admitted I had made a discovery. Not long after, I actually met her at dinner at W. L. George's house in Hamilton Terrace, and, I suppose, I must have fallen in love with her. But one does not know these things; or, at any rate, I do not. What was important was to see her again. When, at parting, she asked me to have tea with her one day, I felt that all was not lost.

I waited for the definite invitation; it never came. At last I plucked up my courage and wrote to remind her. Many days after, I had a note from Geneva to say that she had been ill, and had been sent away; but she was better now and was returning, and looked forward to seeing me. I took heart again. I was back in Oxford when, at last, the invitation came. Up I sped to London and climbed up many stairs to her flat in the Grays Inn Road. Then the ice broke, and I spread out my perplexities. I ought to leave Oxford, and I dared not. She listened gravely, then said: 'I think you ought to leave.' And somehow that seemed to decide the question. Though, even now, I cannot tell whether what was decided was that I should come to London, or that I should be near her. These things were inextricably mixed.

But the next step was clear. I went back to my classical tutor—H. F. Fox, whose memory is blessed to those who knew him—and told him that I must go down for good. I had decided to be a journalist. Would he help me by giving me an introduction to J. A. Spender of *The Westminster Gazette?* I knew they were old friends. Fox was in charge of the Latin and Greek verse competitions which were a famous and singular feature of the *Saturday Westminster;* and occasionally I had helped him, when he was ill, by doing a first rough reading of the entries for him. At first he demurred. Wasn't it a bit shabby to back out, when the college had done so much for me? It was; I felt it was. It would have been better if I could have told him that perhaps it wasn't only a job I was after. But I hardly knew it myself. 'Well,' he said at last, 'I suppose I shall have to. Will you promise to come back and take your Schools?' I promised. Then he said: 'Look here! I'd better take you to Spender myself.'

And he did. I turned up, by arrangement, at the *Westminster* office in Salisbury Square, at the hour I came to know so well—at about eleven o'clock when Spender had written his leader for the day, and the whole office seemed to draw a deep breath of calm before the presses began their final racket. Fox had been with him to prepare the way for me. They had concerted one thing. 'You *must* go back and take your Schools,' said Spender sternly. 'You'll regret it for ever if you don't.' Fox's arm was round my shoulder; so I said firmly that I had made my promise and would keep it. Spender's spectacles became benign. 'I can't take you on the staff. But I'll see you earn enough to live on—if you're prepared to do *anything*.' Then he showed me the kind of semi-political paragraphs with which I must begin. 'We pay 7s 6d each for those. I daresay you can turn out two passable ones every day. That should be nearly £5 a week.' He sat down and wrote a cheque for £5. 'And there's a week in advance. And, by the way,' he added, 'you had better come in every Friday morning, when the books are given out for review.'

Katherine Mansfield was waiting for me in a Soho restaurant. She wore a little straw hat, like a white biretta, with a posy of pink rosebuds at the side and a dark blue suit, rather shabby but beautifully cut, with a goffered blouse and goffered edgings to her cuffs. I told my fairy tale, and produced the cheque. She studied it. 'I don't think I've *ever* liked the look of a cheque so much,' she said. Before we parted that evening, she offered me a room in her flat as her lodger.

Hardly had I settled in, when I was summonded to the office by Spender. 'You read German?' A little, I said. 'Can you do two columns on this, by first thing tomorrow?' And he put in my hands two volumes by General von Bernhardi, *Deutschland und der nächste Krieg.* 'Never fail an editor!' drummed desperately in my brain. I said I could. I laboured from six at night to six in the morning with a dictionary, first a summary, then an article: 'The Ethics of Real-Politik', and took it to the office by 7 a.m. And, at noon, there it was, un-cut and unaltered, on the middle page! To complete the wonder, in the next day's *Kölnische Zeitung* was a long abstract of it 'The semi-official (*offiziös*) *Westminster*

Gazette says. . . .' Obviously, the fate of empires might now depend on me.

On Fridays, Walter de la Mare and J. D. Beresford, who were the staff-reviewers, came to the office, and Spender distributed the books to them, while Naomi Royde-Smith, the brilliant editor of *The Saturday Westminster*, stood by and made her suggestions. I stood in the background, and became a deferential dust-bin: a profitable occupation. I had a pile of books, mainly of the sort turned out almost mechanically for the libraries in those days: *Memoirs of the Regency*, *The Loves of Madame de Pompadour*, *The Prince of the Rakes*. (There were a dozen men, working in the British Museum Reading Room, who could and did manufacture three of them a year.) They had to be reviewed in an 'omnibus' column. When I had finished it, I hurried off with them to Thorpe the bookseller, and sold them for about half the published price. That was a blessed source of income.

Very soon—I forget how—I scratched my way into the book page of *The Daily News*, and stumped regularly up the dingy wooden stairs that led to Robert Lynd. He was only assistant literary editor, though he ought to have been the real thing. But the *News* had lately swallowed *The Morning Leader*: and a senior on the *Leader* staff had been put over his head. But he was as kind to me as he dared to be. He pushed a column review my way when he could, and that was a leg-up, for a column in the *News* was signed.

It was easy for a reviewer to make a living in those pre-war days—or how should I have made one? Within

six months, I was earning about £400 a year. Katherine
and I ought to have been comfortable enough. But we
were not. Two-thirds of what we earned went into keeping *Rhythm* going. It was a foolhardy enterprise—'a
daft magazine,' as D. H. Lawrence truly said, 'but the
people are nice,' I hope as truly. But it brought us
friends: Rupert Brooke, Gilbert and Mary Cannan—
why, I wonder did the gifted Gilbert fade out so cata-
strophically?—the wise and slyly humorous Frank
Swinnerton, the Lawrences, Eddie Marsh the debonair
and generous, the passionate and tempestuous genius,
Henri Gaudier-Brzeska. But, apart from the Lawrences,
who became more than friends and convulsed our lives,
my abiding loyalties in those pre-war London years are
fixed on de la Mare and Beresford. Beresford is now
almost forgotten; but he had the rare and unforgettable
gift of taking a serious young man seriously. And de la
Mare did even more. He took one as though it were a
matter of course, into his world. 'What, if I say
Oxyrhynchus, do you see?' One made a sudden sideways step, and it certainly wasn't papyri.

Yet London disappointed us. Katherine used to sing
a darkie song:

London's no place for me—and I don't like London
    town.

London societee—has turned me down.

and it expressed our feelings. Perhaps it was that we
had bitten off far more than we could chew, in trying to
keep *Rhythm* alive. It was losing nearly £30 a month.
But our pride was involved. Katherine had left *The New
Age* to join it and me; and *The New Age* was venomous

about us. Every number of *Rhythm*, which was by now improving, was systematically torn to pieces in a column or two of *The New Age*. To give up in the face of that was ignominious. We struggled on and impoverished ourselves; and being poor, we cut ourselves off.

It was only with others who lived as precariously as we, like the Gaudiers and the Lawrences, that our defences really went down. And then we found that they had no more liking for London than we had ourselves. The Gaudiers would have done anything to get out of it; and the Lawrences never belonged to it. That republic of art, which I had entered in Paris, where it made no odds if one lived on two shillings a day, and it cost only fourpence to talk for hours in a café, had no counterpart in London. The Café Royal belonged to a different world; it was not a place for the poor.

Not that we were unhappy in our isolation. We had our pub—the Duke of York off Theobald's Road— where the landlady, convinced that we were on the halls and down on our luck, had a motherly habit of giving us two drinks for the price of one. And our isolation gave a curious intensity to the few personal relations we did make. At last, we felt, the need for play-acting was over —for the time, anyhow. The vague thing we were after and called Truth seemed then to come much nearer, and to be almost a city one might inhabit. But it was not at all like London. Probably it was not like Paris, either; but Paris was less of a caricature of the dream.

So, at the first opportunity, we escaped from London into the country: only to discover we could not make a living there. One had, it seemed, to be on the spot. One was too young and expendable not to be easily forgotten. But worse than that, there was a financial catastrophe. The beatific arrangement by which a publisher had taken over *Rhythm* and paid us £10 a month for editing it, on the strength of which we had taken a house in the country, collapsed within three months. The publisher was bankrupt. And, since there was no agreement in writing, his creditors had the assets, and we the debts. Defeated, we returned to London, as to a prison.

Christopher Isherwood

I DON'T remember exactly how or when I first came to London; it was probably while I was still a baby, on a visit to my grandmother. She had a flat at the lower end of Buckingham Street in the Adelphi, overlooking the old water-gate, and for many years this seemed to me to be the very hub of the city. On entering, you breathed in the fine dust of potpourri and the musk of my grandmother's furs: the odour was like an incense offered before the divinity of Sarah Bernhardt, whom she adored and constantly spoke of, and it came to evoke for me the whole magic of the theatre, past and present. At the same time, the watercolours and etchings on her sitting-room walls—of Venice, Granada, Avignon and the Panama Canal—quickened my earliest longings to travel and made me see London as a gateway to the world. Reclining in a deck-chair on the roof of this flat, during the first Great War, my grandmother liked to watch the daylight raids through her lorgnette. No doubt she described the Enemy as 'odious creatures'; it was her favourite phrase of condemnation—and she was later to apply it, in the singular, to George Moore, as she tore from a copy of *The Brook Kerith* the pages she considered blasphemous. She kept the rest of the book, however, because she greatly admired his descriptions of the Holy Land. She was the grandest *grande dame* I have ever known.

As a young man, I lived in London myself; and left it and came back to it often. But, of all these returns, I think that only one will remain with me vividly for the rest of my life. It is my return from the United States at the beginning of 1947. I had been away from England for eight years, almost to the day.

On January 21, around noon, our plane took off from New York. It was nearly dark when we reached New-foundland and circled over the snow-woods and the frozen lakes to Gander, a tiny sprinkle of lights in the wilderness. Transatlantic air travel was somewhat more of an adventure in those days, and less elegantly con-ducted. The big bare white waiting-hall, with its table of simple refreshments, seemed very much a frontier-post; here were the last cup of coffee and the last bun in the Western Hemisphere.

I didn't sleep at all, that night. Not because I was unduly nervous; it was rather a kind of awe that kept me awake. If you are old enough, as I am, to remember Blériot—not to mention Lindbergh— it seems incred-ible to find yourself actually flying the Atlantic. I sat at my little window with its doll's house curtains, vibrat-ing with the changing rhythms of the aircraft and peering out for glimpses of the stars. Fragments of ice, dislodged from the wings, kept rattling against the pane. The cabin was dark, except for a few pin-rays of light from overhead reading lamps. Although all the seats around me were occupied, I felt curiously alone—for the journey I was making was back through time rather than for-ward through space, and it concerned no one on board except myself.

And then—in palest saffron, in pink, in scarlet, in stabbing gold—the sunrise. It gleamed dully on our wet metal and on the cloudfield below us, which was blue-grey like dirty snow. We were flying over an arctic aerial landscape; weirdly solid, with terraces, erosions, valleys and great rounded rugged hills. The roar of our engines, which had been so loud through the night, now sank, or seemed to sink, to a soft hushing sigh. We were gradually coming lower. The plane skimmed the cloud-drifts like a motor-boat, and you had a sudden terrific sense of speed and impact, as though it would surely be dashed to pieces. We raced over them, through them, with the thick vapour whirling back in shreds from our propellers, massing, towering above us, bursting upon us in furious silent breakers. Then, through a wide rift, we saw Ireland—a country of bogs and stony fields, green and mournful in the showery morning, crossed by the winding estuary of the Shannon.

A few miles up the Shannon is Limerick, where I had lived for three years, as a little boy, because my father was stationed there. In those days, it now seems to me, I accepted our unwelcomeness as a matter of course; it didn't seem particularly shocking to me that children of my own age should spit and shout 'dirty Protestant!' as I walked down the street, or that my father's regiment should occasionally be sniped at from rooftops on its march to church.

And now the green and orange flag of independence fluttered over the airport hangars, and an announcement in Gaelic was coming through the loudspeakers as we entered the dining-room. But if the political situation had changed, the local atmosphere had not. I encountered, with happy recognition, the faded grandeur of velvet curtains and the breakfast of under-cooked, disembowelled sausage, and strong but tepid tea. In a brogue as rich as a 'cello, my waiter described the terrible accident of a few weeks back—pointing, as he did so, to the fuselage of the wrecked plane which could still be seen sticking out of a bog beside the airfield. 'The minute I set eyes on them coming down—Mother of God, I said to myself, they're all lost entirely!' His charming, sympathetic eyes were moist and sparkling with enjoyment of his story.

And now, for the first time in my life, I began to feel American—or, at any rate, more American than European. Standing at the bar with a fellow passenger, a businessman from New Jersey, I watched the other travellers and suddenly found myself seeing them through his eyes. There was a group of tweedy foxhunting ladies who didn't look as if they were going anywhere in particular; they might well have stopped in here for a drink after a meet. There was a party of Italian emigrants who had been waiting twenty-four hours to take off for the States; when their plane was announced, they embraced each other and cheered. And there was Sir Somebody Someone, who appeared to be running the British Empire single-handed. He had crossed the Atlantic with us, and was now in an audible state of impatience because we were delayed by the weather and London's failure to 'open'. 'They're waiting for me in Whitehall,' he kept repeating. 'All I can say is, I intend to be in India on Monday.' I was afraid he might have

sufficient authority to order our departure, regardless
of the risk. But it seemed that he hadn't.

When we finally started, it must have been near two
o'clock in the afternoon. We climbed steeply into the
clouds and saw no more land until the coast of the
Bristol Channel. This was my first opportunity to com-
pare bird's eye views of England and the States. What
a contrast between the vast rectangular sections of the
Middle West and the jigsaw pattern of this countryside!
Even from the air, one gets a sense of the complexity of
the past—of the Domesday Book. And of smallness.
How small and vulnerable it all looks—wide open to
the bitter east wind of History! The churches and the
little towns, where three or four straggling roads con-
verge as if expressly to lead a bomber to its target. The
all-too-evident factories and landing strips. An eighteenth century country house with a portico, standing
out tiny but sharply distinct against a wood in which
clearings have been cut to form the initials G.V.R.
We flew quite low, beneath the overcast; and it was
cosy, like a room in the winter light of teatime. London
appeared, a long smudge of brown haze, far ahead. The
plane landed at Bovington Airport.

Here was the scenery of the war—but already it was
falling into disuse. Weeds were growing from cracks in
the concrete runways; the Army signposts and the camou-
flage on the hangars were weather-beaten and faded.
Some Germans were strolling around with spades on
their shoulders—no longer with the air of prisoners but
of accepted inhabitants. And here were the representa-
tives of officialdom; an elderly gentleman and a young

lady doctor of birdlike cheerfulness, waiting to examine us and our belongings in a draughty hut with an iron stove. The lady doctor was sorry I had no certificate of vaccination, but remarked consolingly: 'Oh well, never mind—you've got a jolly good sunburn!' I told her that I'd been swimming in the Pacific, three days before. I could scarcely believe it myself.

Throughout the years I had spent in Hollywood, I had never tired of protesting against the American film presentation of English life. What caricature! What gross exaggeration! But now—and increasingly during the weeks that followed—I began to reverse my judgement. *Is* it possible to exaggerate the Englishness of England? Even the bus which took us from the airport into London seemed grotesquely 'in character'; one almost suspected that it had been expressly designed to amaze foreign visitors. By nature a single-decker, it had had a kind of greenhouse grafted insecurely on to its back. Riding in this was much more alarming than flying. We whizzed down narrow lanes with barely room enough to pass a pram, scraping with our sides the notorious English hedgerows; then slowed with a jerk to circle a roundabout—an Alice-in-Wonderland death trap guaranteed to wreck any driver doing more than five miles an hour. And then we would pass through an English village complete with a village church in a country churchyard; so absurdly authentic that it might have been lifted bodily off a movie-lot at M-G-M. . . . And as for the accents that I now began to hear around me—I could scarcely trust my ears. Surely they were playing it *very* broad? Half of the population appeared to

C.T.L.—H

be talking like Richard Haydn as a Cockney bank clerk, the other half like Basil Rathbone as Sherlock Holmes.

I saw little of London that night, for I went straight to John Lehmann's house; and there a welcome awaited me that I shall never forget. Looking around me at the faces of my old friends, I discovered a happy paradox—namely that, while England seemed fascinatingly strange, my friends and our friendship seemed to be essentially what they had always been, despite the long separation. That was what was to make my visit so wonderful and memorable.

During my re-exploration of London, I got two strong impressions; of shabbiness and of goodwill. The Londoners themselves were shabby—many of them stared longingly at my new overcoat—and their faces were still wartime faces, lined and tired. But they didn't seem depressed or sullen. This may sound like a stupidly sweeping statement by a casual visitor; but I have seen a thoroughly depressed nation—the German in 1932. The English were not in the least like that. For instance, the girls at the ration board, which surely must have been the most exasperating of jobs, were quite gratuitously pleasant. 'It seems so silly', one of them remarked to me, 'to have to call Americans *aliens.*' And this wasn't just a chance encounter with a solitary xenophile, for I heard another girl being extremely sympathetic to a native lady with an obviously unreasonable grievance. On another occasion, when I was on a train, a young couple sat next to me who were about to emigrate to Australia; their baggage, already labelled for the voyage, proclaimed this fact. The other passengers in my compartment congratulated the couple on their decision and questioned them eagerly about their plans—all this without the slightest hint of bitterness or criticism. Of course, this goodwill was somewhat of the grin-and-bear-it variety which is produced by national emergencies; but it had certainly made London a much friendlier place for a stranger to visit. The only negative aspect of it was, perhaps, that the English had become a little too docile in their attitude toward official regulations. 'We're a nation of queue-formers,' someone said. I experienced the truth of this for myself, one afternoon, when I went to a cinema, found that the film I wanted to see had five minutes left to run, and decided to wait outside till it was over. When next I turned my head, I saw that a line of half a dozen people had grown behind me.

London's shabbiness was another matter; it didn't seem to me to have a cheerful side. The actual bomb damage gave you a series of sudden shocks—as when, one evening, I spent some time ringing the doorbell of a house, until I happened to look up through the fanlight and saw that the place was an empty shell, smashed wide open to the stars. Yet the shabbiness was more powerfully and continuously depressing. Plaster was peeling from even the most fashionable squares and crescents; hardly a building was freshly painted. In the Reform Club, the wallpaper was hanging down in tatters. The walls of the National Gallery showed big unfaded rectangles, where pictures had been removed and not yet rehung. Many once stylish restaurants were now reduced to drabness and even squalor. The shortage of materials made all but the most urgent repairs illegal. I heard some weird tales of builders who were smuggled into private homes in their Sunday suits as 'guests', and who didn't emerge until their 'visit'—with much record playing to drown the noise of hammering—was over. London's shabbiness was so sad, I thought, because it was unwilling—quite unlike the cheerful down-at-heel air of some minor Latin American capital. London remembered the past and was ashamed of its present appearance. Several Londoners I talked to at that time believed it would never recover. 'This is a dying city,' one of them told me.

Few of my English readers will need to be reminded that this was the winter of the coal shortage and the great blizzards. The snow started about a week after my arrival; and it soon assumed the aspect of an invading enemy. Soldiers turned out to fight it with flamethrowers. The newspapers spoke of it in quasi-military language: 'Scotland isolated', 'England Cut in Half'. Even portions of London were captured; there was a night when no taxi driver would take you north of Regent's Park. With coal strictly rationed, gas reduced to a blue ghost and electricity often cut off altogether, everybody in England was shivering. I remember how the actors played to nearly empty houses, heroically stripped down to their indoor clothes, while we their audience huddled together in a tight clump, muffled to the chins in overcoats, sweaters and scarves. I remember a chic lunch party composed of the intellectual *beau monde*, at which an animated discussion of existentialism was interrupted by one of the guests exclaiming piteously: 'Oh, I'm so *cold!*' Two or three of my friends said to me then: 'Believe us, this is worse than the war!' By which I understood them to mean that the situation couldn't by any stretch of the imagination be viewed as a challenge to self-sacrifice or an inspiration to patriotism; it was merely hell.

Nevertheless, I have to confess, with the egotism of a tourist, that the blizzard did a great deal to 'make' my visit. It gave me a glimpse of the country in crisis which helped me to some faint idea of what the war years had been like. And, besides this, the cold certainly increased one's energy and sharpened one's senses. There was a great deal to be seen in London that winter—particularly in the art galleries, where many new and talented painters were exhibiting. It was then that I acquired, though only to a very modest degree, the good habit of buying pictures.

My departure was sad, but enlivened by some moments of excitement. For the *Queen Elizabeth*, on which I was to sail for New York, had just run aground on a shifting sandbank called The Brambles while entering Southampton Water. It was thought that she might repeat the accident on her outbound voyage. She didn't, but we all held our breaths as we moved over the danger spot and the brown churned water showed the narrowness of our scrape.

So ended my most memorable visit to London. Since then, I have returned three times—in 1948, in 1952, and again this year—and always with great happiness. But still —it is not quite the same. That precious sense of strangeness and discovery is lost. I doubt if I shall ever get it back.

Alan Pryce-Jones

I LEFT the house, I remember, feeling extremely low.
My father had that morning had a letter from the President of Magdalen College, Oxford, stating shortly
that he thought it a great waste of time and money to
return me to his care after I had been rusticated for a
term. Breakfast had not been easy. My father pointed
out that I was now unemployable. The colonies would
not have me, because I had made it abundantly plain
that I wouldn't work. I could never marry, because
women would find out in time what the President of
Magdalen thought about me. I couldn't join a club, for
the same reason. My father refused to restore my
allowance, which had been cut down, some months before, to an occasional pound note in an envelope. I left
the house, therefore, feeling like Mélisande at one of
those flat, passionless moments when she simply says,
'Je ne suis pas heureuse.'

In Trafalgar Square I met a friend. He was struck by
my plight, and suggested going to see J. C. Squire, who
was having his hair cut in the National Liberal Club.
How my friend knew this I have never divined; but so it
was; and half an hour later I had been appointed assistant editor, unpaid, of *The London Mercury*. Exactly how
Squire knew of my existence I cannot remember either.

118

Somehow or other, I suspect, he had been caught into
the cat's cradle of activity on my behalf which had been
strung together by despairing uncles and parents ever
since I made it plain that I had no vocation to become an
officer in the Brigade of Guards. They wanted me to be
safely at work drafting company orders or scribbling on
sand-tables; but they knew their duty, and behind my
back they sent my crabbed and (alternatively) saccharin
verses to Garvin and Belloc and Squire in the hope of
getting profitable advice.

The following Monday, therefore, I set off to the
Strand. The *London Mercury* office stood just opposite the
Law Courts, in one of two houses which had been
spared by the Great Fire of London. You went into a
little dark passage and up a staircase, past the room
where Mr Pink, the advertising manager, reigned, and,
a half-flight further, you found a small room largely
filled by a large double desk, for Squire and myself.
Upstairs again there was a room for Grace Chapman,
the secretary on whom much depended—whether it was
the eviction of bores, the buying of a buttonhole for the
editor, or advice straight from the shoulder. And somewhere, among back files and trestle-tables and glue-pots
there was usually room for some neophyte upon whom
Squire had laid a protecting hand: I see these neophytes
rolled into one—for they had common denominators.
Their age was a little more than mine: that is, they had
turned twenty. They were girls; they all had reddish
hair; they looked like Rossetti drawings; and they were
—what is by no means universal in offices—all
delightful.

The *London Mercury* office was not like other offices, however. In fact, it was more like a house-party than an office. I suppose there were typewriters (Grace Chapman had one), and ink-pots—but empty—and stationery, and balance-sheets. But I associate the small room with the physical presence of Squire, with MSS, and with visitors. First, the presence. It was to me, at the opposite side of the table, absorbing. Squire used to come up the dark passage at a running walk; he used to slump back into his chair, and he used to start a conversation at once. It was extremely good conversation—so good that it is his voice I remember, to the exclusion of everything else, except a pair of thick spectacles, and a fuzz of hair set on brown, wind-tanned skin. There would be ash about, and an eruption of paper. But the small details vanish in a general impression of vivacity, of kind candour, of a sort of obstinate manliness. The time I speak of is 1928—the end, that is, of a soaring, stamping period in English letters. The writers of my generation brushed their hair carefully, drank cocktails, liked lifts in cars, read German, smoked Russian cigarettes rolled in black paper, and generally affected a very delicate approach to the art of living. By contrast, the writers of Squire's generation looked considerably blown about by the wind; they drank beer, walked like Meredith, they hated German, and their curtains reeked of pipe-smoke. Squire, therefore, although he was still a youngish man, seemed to me to possess a dinosaur quality: a dinosaur of rare tact, discrimination, and bounty. He must have thought me and my friends, with our talk of Rilke and Büchner, ridiculous in the extreme.

But he never betrayed the fact by so much as an in-
flexion. And when, at the earliest possible moment, we
went off together to the Temple Bar, the pub next door,
I almost felt myself capable of rising to the occasion
while our visitors came streaming in: Belloc in flowing
cape, and Beachcomber and sometimes Edmund
Blunden; Hugh Mackintosh and Moray McLaren, my
predecessor; perhaps, too, some guarded young man,
feeling his way, like Stephen Spender or Wystan Auden.
The occasion at any rate was less difficult than sometimes in the country where I used to go and stay with
the Squires.

These visits were marked by Squire's extraordinary
accident-proneness. I remember, for instance, once in
front of Godalming station an old lady caught the end
of her umbrella between his spectacles and his nose. She
wrenched them off, and I had to be driven at speed in
an enormous Buick, shaped like a boat, knowing that
Squire could not see the end of the bonnet. And an incident which might have ended even more disastrously
marked a shooting-expedition near Edinburgh when he
shot a pheasant in a high wind, looked round in triumph,
and a few seconds later was knocked unconscious by the
bird falling on his head. And there were moments of
social embarrassment, too, like a crowded party after a
cricket-match in early autumn at which I was asked
whether I would sooner share a single bed with an
elderly stranger, or put up a hammock on the lawn,
beset by dew and earwigs. Or sheer inadequacy, as when
I was woken one morning, after rather a heavy night, by
Squire in Rosslyn Park stockings shouting up from the

garden, 'Coming out for a kick-out?' and after I had
answered 'No', I lay in bed and heard the thump of one
boot on ball, and an occasional tinkle of glass followed
by a beautifully placed oath thrown up, though he must
have been face downward, from the ruins of cloche or
cucumber-frame.

No, there can never have been a kinder master than
Jack Squire, nor a more generous one. The *London
Mercury* was far from rich. Indeed, by the time the
editor's buttonhole had been bought from some special
vendor in the street the till was usually empty, as those
contributors who came down to the office in quest of
their money found to their cost. Still, we seem always
to have been setting off, in a taxi, to the Connaught
Rooms for lunch, in parties of six or eight, with James
Bone and Archie Macdonnel to delight us, and sometimes a distinguished visitor from abroad—I remember
the white head of Robert Frost especially vividly—to
make the excuse for an extra bottle of claret.

Why the paper came out, or rather, how it came out,
was mysterious, owing to the conflict of energies in the
building. For one thing, there was Squire's *Observer*
article to get written, and I still have an anxious impression of messengers from Tudor Street lurking
among the palms of the Temple Bar, while he, un-
ruffled beside his glass of red wine (for this was a time
in which he had decided to drink nothing but wine, on
the grounds that wine is less extravagant than whisky
and less filling than beer), and sustaining two conver-
sations at once, corrected a galley at lightning speed
and with undeviating accuracy. Then there were the

neophytes, who made sudden muddles of the kind which involve subsequent visits of apology. And above all there were the visitors.

Some, like that angular and unjustly forgotten poet, John Freeman, came for a purpose, did what they had to do and left. Most expected a drink, if not a lunch; and— as in all newspaper offices—quite a lot were merely dotty. One in particular I remember: a prosperous-looking woman who greeted me as an old friend. In a moment, she said, she would remember where we had met. Yes, she had it. That time on the Arno, in a boat with Piero della Francesca. And then, having established our friendship, she turned briskly to the matter in hand: something to do with saving Stonehenge, it probably was, or with defeating the Bishop of London's plans for destroying the Wren churches (for even then the ecclesiastical authorities, unless carefully watched, ripped down any good building which inconvenienced their financial arrangements). It was one of Squire's admirable qualities that he saw each of the arts through eyes entirely unaffected by fashion. At a time, therefore, when respectable opinion conceived that the kind of building which needed preservation was limited to some crumbling setting for pyx and ambry, he acted vigorously to save what could be saved of the seventeenth and eighteenth centuries, and a very little later, when I brought John Betjeman into the life of the *London Mercury*, he was among the first to see the point of Keble College, or Scarisbrick, of All Saints, Margaret Street.

These activities, however, were not directly concerned with editing. And there, month by month, we

were, with nothing in the till, and Mr Pink looking
almost sombre (though he could never quite achieve
that), and the neophytes leaving the proofs in buses, and
I myself, jaded beyond bearing by long hours at the bar,
by the discovery of life in every context possible to a
nineteen-year-old without much conscience, and by far
too much conversation; there was I, trying to snatch a
few moments of peace and quiet in the only restful part
of the building—a small attic lavatory, where I would
shut myself up with a pile of the day's manuscripts.
Every now and again the situation got quite out of hand,
and an SOS had to be issued to some benefactor like
Lord Lee of Fareham. Always, at the last second, help
came; but I doubt if we ever perceived how directly that
help was due to the disinterested and unflagging energy
of Squire himself. He took no salary; he had no literary
axe to grind; and most of his time (in retrospect) seems
to have been given to showing kindness to others: putting broadcasts in our way, introducing us to American
publishers, and so forth. Yet the back files show that
year after year he managed to produce a paper which at
some time or other must have printed almost every good
English writer of the day, and quite a number of them
for the first time.

This was all the harder to achieve because of the
sharp divisions in the literary London of the late 1920s.
I think I may have been more aware of these divisions
than some of my friends owing to the fact that I fell between two groups of writers. To take only the Oxford
stars, older than me there were prodigious figures like
Evelyn Waugh and Cyril Connolly whom I barely

aspired to know by sight. My exact contemporaries—
Wystan Auden and Stephen Spender—I only came to
know later, owing to my good fortune (as I soon saw it
to be) in getting sent down from Magdalen. We were
all more or less part of a single figure in the carpet. And
though some of us were on excellent terms with Bloomsbury, and others on excellent terms with the Sitwells,
we were aware that *they* represented other figures again.
All in all, however, our figures were drawn together into a single design. We felt ourselves part of something
new, and distinct from the world of Belloc, Baring,
Wells, Bennett. Their carpet was not our carpet, in fact.

Yet day by day, to the Temple Bar, emissaries from
these different worlds came amicably together. And
although some of the great chams who ruled the opposed
school of writing scoffed at Squire and the *Mercury*,
they sent their manuscripts along like the rest, to be
stacked in a huge white drawer under the window or
(when they slipped behind the drawer) to be lost from
one year's end to the next, like the original of Belloc's
Belinda, which lay in limbo for a whole lustre until
Desmond MacCarthy printed it elsewhere just at the
moment we found it.

Anything might happen in that room. I remember
coming on the galley of *Ulysses*, less one or two which
had been burned on moral grounds. For it happened that
Squire had admired some of Joyce's earlier work and had
asked him to send his next book in proof, to be sure of a
really prompt review. It was not, I gathered what he
had expected when it came. Even the paranormal reared
its head from time to time. Soon after I had been

remembered in my fifteenth-century Florentine boat with Piero della Francesca, a poet abroad—was he not called Bransford?—sent in some poems after a long silence. I remember Grace Chapman bringing them down, and exclaiming, 'But I thought he was a corpse,' while Squire, telling me about him, doodled on the blotting-paper. And then, as soon as it could reach us a postcard came from Switzerland, bearing on it nothing but a distich:

> Bransford, believed a 'corpse,' yet heard
> Your pencil when it wrote the word.

And there, on the pad, the word still lay before us.

So the years passed pleasantly enough: arranging cricket-matches, in which there seemed usually to be eight on one side and fourteen on the other, making no allowance for those who took the wrong train; gossiping in the Adelphi with Jimmy Stern, who ended by doing most of my work for me; getting interviewed by a high official of the BBC in Savoy Hill, and having the opening question shot at me, 'Do you believe in God?'; and above all following Squire round, to Lady Ottoline's, perhaps, or even down to see Robert Bridges on Boar's Hill, while always a taxi ticked up outside, and always there was one more baroque curve of conversation to be rounded before it was time to go.

I can say farewell to the *Mercury* most easily on the occasion of the Squire dinner. Somewhere about 1930, it was thought by a number of his friends that Squire ought to be given a dinner at the Dorchester. It fell to us, however, to carry out the organization. And for anxious days we rushed up and down stairs, while the neophytes made up table-plans which had at once to be scrapped, as a late-coming ambassadress or the President of the Royal Academy unexpectedly entered their names. More and more claret was drunk at the bar. Less and less time was left for anything but questions of *place-ment*. We never thought we should get ourselves, and the subscribers and the hero of the evening all together into the banqueting-room on the right day. But we did it. And when Squire rose to answer the toast—not without a catch in the voice—I hope we overcame our proper respect for the Dorchester sufficiently to cheer and stamp with a quarter of the warmth we felt when we caught his eyes beaming behind their round thick glasses.

William Sansom

CHUFF, chuff, *chuff*—and what is implied here must be a first sight of the platform labelled L for Literature, with its Refreshment Saloons, its Station-Masters' Offices and other conveniences—a fairly gloomy stretch of promenade, here and there illuminated brightly by both gas and electricity, a few sodium lamps, even a silver candelabra or two; a place where much waiting is done. My own journey thither seems to have been by a series of slow trains travelling by wrong routes, often running backwards, and occasioning thus a fairly late arrival.

I had been to London before. Having spent a child-hood in Streatham, where I must have dawdled up Thrale Road a thousand times but never heard the name Johnson mentioned, we moved out into Surrey proper, into a new house in what is known as Stockbroker's Country, but which is really peopled by a diversity of moderately affluent men in anything from fuller's earth to gutta percha, sponge-importers and the like: but the top of the tree being what it is, they might as well have been stockbrokers, and the tree was certainly a Surrey pine. The address was Woodland Way, the Warren, Kingswood.

Down Woodland Way one early, cold, dark morning in winter some years later I set off, bowler-spatted, for

my first taste of the 8.05 and London Bridge. I was
18, and entering an Anglo-German commercial bank
to begin my commercial training. My right foot
plodded across the Bridge towards the bank; my left
kicked out at the West End, for whose entertainment I
was busy designing numbers of songs and lyrics and
sketches, none of which ever saw the light of night.
However, for the next four years I handled other
people's money, usually in the form of bonds and shares.
I wince now to remember how, as a trusted messenger,
I once dropped £10,000 worth of negotiable bearer
bonds in Lombard Street, which a thoughtful passer-by
had to pick up for me: I sweat to think of the mornings
in charge of the dollar-bond-market telephone where I
easily made some thousands of pounds between ten and
noon, buying and selling other people's bonds. The
bank was altogether a slap-up affair, plenty of marble
and oxidized copper. I shall always remember the
managers and directors as kind, courteous and gentle.
They were Jewish; frockcoats and braided jackets and
carnations were worn; directorial desks were inlaid with
mother-of-pearl; and the president, an old man of ivory
with his feet wrapped in a travelling rug, spared the
time on several occasions for a private hour's talk when,
between the violets in his buttonhole and the scent of his
brown Havana, the white-bearded face, wise and kind
but above all *interested*, told me how one must not think
of Chesapeake and Ohio Sinking Fund Debentures as
pieces of paper, but see the railroad in one's mind, think
what it carried, see the bales and judge the need of them
in this town or that. . . . 'And take Rio Tinto,' he said,

C.T.L.—I

'it's not just a copper mine. *It's one of the biggest holes in the world.*' This naturally put a touch of the right colour into banking—the lists of shares began to live in much the same way as postage-stamp collecting evokes thoughts of exotic origins—but it was no good. My left foot was kicking too hard. And in my capacity of information-officer I would be writing to one of my financial interests with half my mind still oomp-boomping away at a lyric:

> My dear Sir So and So. . . . Wiggins Teape showed a net profit for 1932-3 of. . . . the moon was melancholy and so was I. . . Peruvian Tramways $ Debs . . . you're a moonful of mink, you're the kitchen sink. . . Babcocks, Wilcox. . . .

Finally I managed to have a waltz performed, by devious pressures, at, of all places, the Folies Bergères in Paris. I never went to hear it, I have often wondered what it might have looked like; but I was in London, though just about then I left the bank and went into an advertising agency as copywriter.

None of this may seem to have much to do with the literary platform; but we are just in sight of the first signal-boxes: and I mention these other matters at some length to emphasize what had hitherto been, and was really to continue as, a most circuitous route, single line suburban, with even the destination inprecise. The point I must make is delay, and braking—even the lack of any *practical* reason to leave a comfortable Philistine entourage for a completely unknown world of what one may call Art. It might have been different had the home been ruled by a Victorian hand of iron: but it was unoppressive, and also there was in a way Art about, for my father was a Sunday painter, and this may have suggested to me that Art was a pleasure rather than a devotion.

Before starting to write songs, I had always as a child written stories and verse. The verse was modelled on bits from *Punch* and things hanging about the house like the *Ingoldsby Legends*. The stories were ghoulish, I think out of Sax Rohmer. They were were oddly constructed. I still have one curious MS that begins breezily as a tale of some terrible Chinaman torturing a Spanish detective, and then the Spaniard begins to talk, and there follow pages and pages of Spanish dialogue carefully copied out of a phrase-book: this must finally have become tiresome, and suddenly breaks off, never to end. However, all these years I had been sitting here and there at tables in rooms writing. I wrote the first act of an operetta, and I wrote rather more grown-up stories, and finally a few awful poems (it is cruel to say that; but the truly awful part was that they happened so very late in life—I was nearly 24). I had none of the usual thing—the soul-sure desire of the twenties and even the teens to be a Writer. I never ever hoped to be a writer. The world of writers was hopelessly far and high away: it was simply not to be thought of. With Shakespeare and the Bible and all the other classics slain stone dead by the school desk, my reading eschewed *all that* as dull and dry—and my reading was devoted to Pamela Frankau and Michael Arlen, Noël Coward and the texts of a number of contemporary lightish plays. By chance, I cannot think how, Virginia Woolf swam into the middle of this on *The Waves*, was violently appreciated, but never followed up. As for writing stories, I only half hoped to see one published in a popular magazine, nothing more than that. It is difficult to realize how completely cut off from the rest of the world a comfortable rugger-bred middle-class youth can be. The serious arts are something godly and distant, unintelligible and a bit dotty. Although by nature the bent in me was always mildly original and revolutionary, I was these things in a vacuum: worse, I felt I was wrong, that the established order was right, that I had let everybody and everything down. In such cases— and the point of this account is really to suggest how very many others like me there must be—what is needed most is some helping hand. These are few, and I had none. The thing was to have a job and make money. Outside this, one could play the goat. My goat was the light theatre and song writing. I intended to play it, but never dreamed of living by its professional milk.

However, it did come about that I left the bank for copywriting, as being a sensible commercial way to use a questionable ability to write. At the same time, I left home for a thirty-bob room round the corner from Shepherd Market and the ghost of the immortal Hispano Suiza and its green hat. Soon I happened to be given, by a red-haired Rumanian lady, a cocktail with ether in it in that very house. This suited me down to the ground. But within a month the ground had unexpectedly shifted.

At the advertising office, my room was changed. I was put in an office-for-two with a strange tall man with an uncombed mop of hair and a long woollen tie. He came in with a kind of breezy, serious gusto, carrying a lot of dangerous-looking thin books, private stuff, poetry. After an affable greeting or two, he turned to write copy about a liver-medicine on the bright yellow paper provided for such purposes. I returned to dealing with a nail-polish remover, literally only, but meanwhile stole a glance or two at the stranger's visionary pale eyes and his suit, which seemed to be made of hair. I had seen nobody like this ever before; or if I had, had averted my smooth little eyes.

At midday this man suddenly turned and said: 'How about some gudfud?' As a new boy I was prepared to agree to anything. But within a couple of hours I had understood exactly what Norman Cameron meant by his soon-to-be-well-known invitation to good food, had met my first poet and been astounded that he laughed and drank, ate and enjoyed life like other people. It was the first of many such lunches. Years later I asked him what on earth had prompted him to bear the company of someone who could only talk of Louis Armstrong and the like, and scarcely understood half he could have said. He answered that it was because in the morning I brought into the office a breath of brandy from the night before—I was helping to run a night-club at the time—and that this was invigorating.

During the next months Norman wrote medicinal copy in the morning and translated Rimbaud in the afternoon. The particular copy consisted of about fifteen exhortative lines that had been tested and retested exhaustively by American market research organizations

and thus proved nearly perfect, so that Norman's job
was simply to find perhaps one substitute word, such as
'happy' for 'good', which sounds absurd but within the
esoteric is important and may make sales differences of
thousands of pounds. So he pondered this problem in
the morning, lunched well, and through the relatively
empty afternoon hours translated Rimbaud and wrote
his own poems. During this time he handed me Rilke,
Rimbaud, even Hemingway and many others like these
that I had never heard of. They clicked, amazingly,
instantly. Plainly the forces of hero-worship were at
work and I was ready to like them—but that does not
explain how I understood them. It is possible that I
simply recognized the antithesis of the academic, and
only thought I understood them. However, when in the
past I had picked up, say, Keats, and tried to combat the
school-curse, I felt too much the How-wonderful-I-am
reading-a-poem feeling, without becoming involved
except for a line here and there, before the old fuzz-
cloud came down and I shut the book. But now I was
certainly involved. Norman also said that Cole Porter
was a true poet. That clinched it.

When the office closed, we would often walk along to
a wineshop where goodish cheap hock was served on
heavy wood tables, and there I met a number of Norman's friends—an astounded cherub called Thomas, a
clerkly-looking fellow called Gascoyne, egg-domed Len
Lye like an ascetic coster in his raffish cap, and many
others whose names I cannot immediately remember
but who, with hock and words, signed and resigned this
new lease to my life. What impressed most was that,

unlike certain other writers *manqués* back in the office, they did not discuss literary theory or whine about their souls and sensitivities—they made up things there and then, grabbed down extraordinary stories and myths from the air, wrote down doggerel and verse. 'I am the short world's shroud, he said'—said Mr Thomas, I remember—'I share my bed with Finchley Road and Foetus.' Not much, you may think. But it was preposterous and euphonious—and if you add the movement of faces and laughter and the hock, the evening smoke and the evening loll-together, and at least the freshness of such a statement—the impact may be guessed at. For until those times I had still thought of a poet as a cartoonist's poet, a sort of gangling sissy dancing among lambs in spring.

There was one difficulty. The Spanish War had begun, and this was naturally much discussed. But not by me. For one thing, I was politically ignorant and innocent—or inane. Is it, I wonder, generally known that the ritual phrase 'Politics, sex and religion barred' was still then, perhaps is now, jovially boomed and enforced before groups of sporting young Englishmen settle down for an evening's jaw? The extent of my political ignorance can be gauged by the fact that I had been in a German-Jewish bank at the time Hitler took over, and beyond an extra bustling in the marble corridors, realized nothing. Earlier, I had been in the market-place in Bonn when a group of Nazis armed with *gummiknüppeln* rushed a group of Communists or workers, had in fact stood in the middle shouting 'Engländer! Engländer!' trying both to elevate my arms in

Kamerad-fashion and point to my chest at the same time, a problem without three hands, before taking to my heels: yet I never bothered to find out what the rumpus was all about. However, the point I am getting to is that my father was a naval architect building ships particularly for the Spanish Navy. Officers from the admiralty in Madrid often visited us, they were good friends of the family, the garden at Kingswood was gay with Spanish captains strolling among the rhododendrons, between bark-bound pigeon-cot and crazy-paved lily-pond. Now news came in daily that these our friends were either in prison or executed. One was reported to have been sawn in half (actually he was an unlikeable man, and there was a certain unspoken double-think in the family at this news). So my own difficulty, with unpolitical attachments to the wrong side and my new friends champing and sneething to get at them, can be understood. Once again I felt wrong, and yet right; but always out on the other side of an extraordinary fence made of bowler-hats and Omar Khayyám, saxophones and golf bags.

This was the only fly in an ointment full of pearls. For instance, there was Thomas and the piano. Sometimes he used to come tumbling up the long stairs to my awful room in Clarges Street and sit down at a small piano I used for composing. He did not know a note from a note. But out of the instrument he wreaked an extemporary sound, Debussy-Bergish—his fingers clutched at the notes and somehow he managed, by instinct for rhythm and tones, a beautiful anarchic disharmony of his own; never absurd, with a beginning and a middle and sometimes a kind of end.

Then one day Norman, always generous and hospitable, always so thoroughly *considerate*, took me to the surrealist exhibition in Burlington Street. Another apocalypse.

I must explain that my father, besides being a naval architect and a kind of commercial traveller in battleships, in and out first of the Czarist and then of the Spanish admiralties, was as well a practised dilettante artist. He was an accomplished copyist in oils and a good draughtsman in his own right. Copies of things in the Tate hung about the house, which itself was furnished in a beguiling mixture of Morris, Maples, art-nouveau and heroic Russian bronzes brought back from St Petersburg. I spent my early years studying Bix Beiderbecke and Co. under the eyes of 'The Laughing Cavalier', which are painted so that they follow you as you move about the room. This must have inoculated me against much academic painting, as school had Shakespeare. And now—here were these surrealists, illustrative, often painting academically too, but at last blowing the old, old story sky-high! I was immediately addicted forever. I was under no delusion that they painted the subconscious: theirs was a plain statement of reality: the umbrella and the sewing machine on the dissecting table was no strange association, what it did was dissociate these objects, which you then saw clearly in their own right for the first time. My way of looking at things was altered. Sitting by an asbestos stove, for instance, I could at last see it straight, without thinking 'stove' and 'asbestos'. It could get up and walk (though

there are dangers here, as with a club near Chalk Farm,
Lottie's indeed, which was done up as a floral garden
with rustic benches yet had five asbestos stoves standing
in a row against one wall, which most members avoided
but to which I became enslaved).

Then I was transferred from copy to the radio-pro-
duction department, started writing dramatic scripts
and producing variety programmes, and slid away from
Norman's influence as easily as it slid my way.

A little later, though, I was given a second chance.
With the war, I joined the Fire Brigade at Kensington,
and by a thousand-to-one fluke got posted to Hampstead, which I had never before even visited. There, of
course, in the station were waiting ready-made painters
and writers. In particular, Leonard Rosoman, whom I
would watch paint for hours in the off-duty moments.
And another gifted man, Fernando Henriques, a scholar
of West Indian extraction, now a lecturer in anthro-
pology, who brought with him into the station a small
but precious private library. Fernando and I shared a
billet. After the first bomb fell, it was impossible to
transfer from the Fire to any other Service—one was
there for good. So we settled our bunks in the basement
boot-room of the Hampstead High School for Girls,
where the detachment was barracked, filled the lockers
with books, and prepared ourselves, when disengaged,
to read out the war. Where plimsolls had been, De
Gourmont now nestled, Mann and Montherlant and
Jung and Jaspers beamed from holes which hockey-
boots had shared with Dr Sloane's liniment and perhaps
Miss Dell's. So, in between actions and exercise and

polishing brass (*very* good for a writer), we lay in the
boothole and there under Fernando's influence I read
and finally started, for the first time seriously, to write.
Two days' monastic company, one day's leave in the
play world. It was an excellent recipe.

Such were the dock and oil fires, we all thought that
it would be a question of weeks if not days before we
were wiped out. This was, of course, what is called a
sobering thought. And for the first time I said to myself:
I must write down something absolutely true. Hitherto,
everything I had written had been directed at an audience, conceived with their entertainment prominently
in view, and had consequently rung false and fussy. So
I wrote a very short story based on an experience in the
bombing. By a purely geographical chance I met someone who lived near and who was then business manager
at *Horizon*, William Makins. He said *Horizon* wanted
stories and why didn't I send them something? The
fence of bowler hats was still well erected, I was still far
on the other side, and so I said don't be silly, they
wouldn't want my kind of thing.

However, I sent in this story. *Horizon* accepted it, it
was published, and as if this were not enough to bowl
me over, I received the gilded sledgehammer blow of
real letters from real book-publishers asking for a book.
It was astonishing and impossible. I started writing
like a racing engine.

A little later Stephen Spender came to be stationed
with us. Again, an established poet friendly and easy to
be with . . . again no resemblance to the unapproach-
able great figure I had still bogged somewhere in my

imagination. He read a few stories I had and told me to send them to *New Writing*. John Lehmann accepted one; and later, others.

'It' had happened again. For what, apart from publication, was so impressive about both these acceptances was that they were conducted impersonally by post, with neither influential meetings nor agent's interventions. Hitherto I had imagined that pretty well everything in the world is arranged by strings pulled, pats on the back, obeisances, percentages, perks. And so it is. But here was an exception. Here, it had to be believed, was an honest situation. Disinterested interest. A fact which was underlined by a number of rejections from both of these editors.

Much later I was invited to drink or dine with Connolly and Lehmann, and to meet what have been called the nobs. The most that I can remember about this, about what is so often condemned as the brittle round of literary parties, is again an overwhelming surprise at being accepted so easily over the Fence, and of holding my tongue like grim death in case I made a gaffe.

There is, in this account, one important cloud excluded. As a child I had always been shy and self-conscious. Then at 17 I lost control of my voice. For about three years I could only either shout, or speak in a whisper. I was, a specialist said, a belly-breather. In a railway carriage, for instance, I could only whisper creepily at my neighbour or bawl, 'COULD YOU GIVE ME A LIGHT PLEASE?' This embarrassment was complicated by a fairly fictitious fear of a poor physique—narrow-chested, round-shouldered, buck-toothed. For years at

school I had exercised privately to combat these condi-
tions, sleeping in terribly contorted chest-expansion
positions, spending hours with my fist rammed against
my teeth to push them in. Even today, with these qualms
somewhat settled, disguised by beard and embonpoint, I
feel more like a bag of artificial gestures moving about
than a body. The upshot was that I spent years, awful
years, from 17 to about 23, as a proper young
paranoiac. I thought all strangers were laughing at me.
I hated to be in a public place. I would, for instance,
seldom walk alone in a peopled street like the Strand or
Piccadilly, but always moved by the parallel back streets.
The remedy was Dutch Courage, and plenty of it.
Although by the time I was 30 these fears were largely
forgotten, there was a residual habit, so that always
before I went to a gathering of this new literary kind I
took care to take aboard a few strong, reassuring drinks.
These, with what afterwards I was given, proved
enough to make me forget by the next morning what
anyone had looked like or what had been said. Rosily
enjoyable it usually was—but more than this I shall
never know.

One thing must be added about those early days so
late in life. When I set in to try to live by writing seriously, with no other job, I saw that the only thing to do
was to save part of any money I earned against the
draughty days, and to lower all costs of living to do this.
There is, I think, no necessary connexion between a
writer and even the lowest present-day accepted standards of living. And what happened? Through the post
from two people unknown to me, who knew nothing of

my circumstances, came gifts of money, sums like £100 and £50 on about six occasions: one anonymously, one insisting on a confidential secrecy.

So there. First, honest interest. Then plain goodness. It makes for faith.

Jocelyn Brooke

I FIRST came to London—in the sense of coming to live there—in 1927, when my father retired from the family business at Folkestone and settled at Blackheath. I was then 18; in the same year I went up to Oxford, only to be sent down, in ignominious circumstances, at the end of the following summer. Thereafter, for several years, I worked intermittently (and wholly without ambition) at a series of menial jobs in the book-trade; but I didn't feel that I was a real Londoner, I had come there by force of circumstances, not from choice, and in any case I lived with my parents in a remote suburb. On my occasional nights out (I couldn't afford many) I would pub-crawl, in a rather gloomy and Byronic fashion, round the shadier bars and night-boxes; at that period I was living largely in a fantasy world whose background owed much to the novels I had lately been reading—Proust, Huxley and the early Waugh—and I was apt to invest real people and real places with a wholly fictitious glamour. Most of my acquaintances were, in fact, rather dull; and, apart from infrequent and mainly abortive excursions into Fitzrovia, I had no contacts at all with the literary world. In 1938 I retired to the country; the war came, I joined up as a private in the Army, and after the war re-enlisted on a short-service

143

engagement. A year later I bought myself out, and, since my first book had proved a flop financially, I began to look round for a job. I found one—with the BBC, as Talks Producer; and though I was by then close on 40, I look upon this as my first real 'coming to London'.

To this day I don't know how or why I obtained the post; my academic qualifications were nil, and the fact that I had published a 'slim' and rather frivolous volume of autobiography could hardly, in itself, have seemed much of a recommendation; nor, for that matter, was my training as a 'Special Treatment' orderly in the RAMC likely to enhance my status as a Talks Producer. I had applied for the job, on a friend's advice, without the faintest hope of getting it; and it was with considerable astonishment that I received, one morning, an invitation to appear before a Selection Board.

It was an alarming prospect, and I arrived for the interview in a state of twittering apprehension. After a longish wait in an ante-room I was ushered, at last, into the presence of the Board. There seemed to be at least twenty of them, male and female, seated round a semicircular table; I was invited by the chairman to sit down; I did so, trying to look a great deal more self-possessed and intelligent than I felt. It was, I fear, a poor effort; aware of the concentrated scrutiny of twenty pairs of eyes, I felt my mouth go dry and my scalp begin to prickle. I was unpleasantly reminded of a recent occasion in the Army, when I had been on a charge for losing my A.B.64 Part I.

'And why, Mr Brooke,' the chairman was asking me, in the polite but rather truculent tone of a prosecuting counsel, 'why exactly do you want to work for the BBC?'

'I suppose,' I mumbled hopelessly, 'because I'm in need of a job.'

'Yes, yes, quite so. . . . But may I ask what made you apply for this *particular* job?'

I was tempted to answer—quite truthfully—that I hadn't the faintest idea; instead, I murmured vaguely that I thought it would be 'rather interesting'.

A pregnant silence ensued, during which the Board digested this singularly lukewarm tribute to the august institution which they represented. The silence was broken at last by another member of the Board, a lady:

'And what was your last job, Mr Brooke?' she asked, with the bright, efficient air of a social welfare officer interviewing some particularly farouche and unco-operative juvenile delinquent.

'I was a Corporal in the RAMC,' I answered firmly and not without a touch of professional pride.

'Ah yes, I see. . . .' The lady consulted, briefly, a file of memoranda upon the table in front of her. 'And what, Mr Brooke,' she brightly pursued, 'did your duties mainly consist of?'

'Treating VD,' I replied.

There was a rustling of note-books; somebody dropped a pencil; the lady's face assumed that expression of resolute, unshakeable tolerance with which sophisticated middle-aged ladies, who grew up in the 'twenties, are wont to greet the more daring sallies of a younger generation.

'Yes, I *see*, Mr Brooke. . . . And now, tell me——'

C.T.L.—K

The inquisition proceeded; other members of the Board chimed in, firing question after question at me with what seemed an almost frivolous inconsequence. In ten minutes it was all over, and I slunk out of the room, convinced that the Board must have firmly decided, by now, that I was a harmless lunatic who had somehow managed to stray into the building by mistake.

A week or two later, to my utter stupefaction, I learned that my application had been accepted, and that I was to report for duty at Broadcasting House on the first of January. Perhaps, I thought, the chairman of the Selection Board had suddenly gone mad; or, possibly, my name had been substituted, by a clerical error, for that of somebody else. The mistake, however, if mistake it was, must have gone undetected by the authorities, for a few weeks later I found myself sitting in an office in the Langham Hotel, in the company of an extremely sympathetic (though alarmingly efficient) secretary, twiddling my thumbs and wondering what on earth I was supposed to do next.

Presumably, I thought, being a Talks Producer, I was expected to produce talks: but how—and where from? They could hardly, after all, be produced out of a hat. My colleagues in the Talks Department had assured me that it was all quite simple, really, once one got the hang of things. . . . In just such jaunty and encouraging tones had the maths master at my prep school sought to convince me of the essential 'simplicity' of quadratic equations; I remained now—as I had remained then—entirely unconvinced.

'They'll be allotting you some spaces soon, I expect,' said my secretary, who was busily employed in re-arranging an enormous filing cabinet whose serried folders were as yet virginally unsullied by so much as a single document. 'Of course,' she went on, pursuing an earlier train of thought which some remark of mine had interrupted, 'it's useless trying to read Kafka in transla-tion—one loses the whole flavour of his style.'

Doubtless, I thought, my secretary was right—not only about Kakfa (a subject upon which, since I didn't know German, I was unable to pronounce judgement) but about the spaces as well. Meanwhile, despite a recur-rent sense of guilt, I found myself mildly enjoying the incongruous situation in which I found myself. I had never before possessed an office—let alone a secretary —of my own, and the fact that I had, as yet, nothing whatever to do tended to emphasize rather than to diminish the sense of self-importance engendered by my novel surroundings. Sprawling in my revolving chair, behind a man-sized desk, I could imagine myself a brisk and efficient technocrat, a kind of highbrow tycoon; it was all very agreeable, and I had never felt so grand in my life.

'. . . and just *look* at Sartre,' my secretary exclaimed, rousing me abruptly from my Balchinesque dream of myself as a kind of cultural back-room boy, 'you must admit that he reads *frightfully* badly in English.'

Plainly, I couldn't expect to inhabit for much longer such a delightful fool's paradise; spaces, all too soon, were allotted to me, documents began to trickle—

though still in quite manageable quantities—into the
filing cabinet, and my visions of myself as a brilliant and
revolutionary technocrat became progressively blurred
by the quotidian preoccupations of a very junior and less
than usually gifted member of the Talks Department.
My job didn't, after all, prove to be so very exacting:
far less so than quadratic equations, and one couldn't
after all—whatever ghastly solecisms one might com-
mit—be beaten; nor was the Head of the Talks Department—though held in considerable awe by his subor-
dinates—nearly so alarming a figure as the Headmaster
of St Ethelbert's.

The process by which a talk was produced was largely
a matter of routine: one was allotted a space of fifteen
or twenty minutes—either in the Home, Light or Third
—which one was then responsible for filling by a given
date, usually several weeks ahead. Having decided upon
a suitable topic and a speaker qualified to talk about it,
one's job was to commission the talk, edit the script and,
in due course, rehearse the speaker and put him on the
air. One's choice of subject and performer was, of course,
subject to approval by the Head of the Talks Department, and too often my suggestions would be firmly
rejected: for the most part they tended to be too frivolous or (a favourite BBC word) too 'marginal'. In
time, however, I learnt without too much difficulty
to adapt my ideas to the *via media* prescribed by the
Corporation. Such purely intellectual difficulties were,
indeed, far less worrying than the actual physical process of putting a speaker on the air: congenitally hopeless at gadgets, I spent my first few weeks roaming

round the studios and trying to master—with the help
of my colleagues—the intricacies of the various switches
which enable the producer to establish liaison between
the studio itself and the control-room adjoining. Offici-
ally, this is a job for the programme-engineer, and a
producer is justified in adopting a somewhat lordly
attitude towards such base trivialities; there is always a
chance, though, that the programme-engineer may fail
to turn up—a disaster which did, in fact, happen to me
more than once during my brief career, and which
remains for me to this day a recurrent source of
nightmare.

On one such occasion I had arranged to rehearse a
book-talk by that admirable critic Mr Walter Allen.
Installed within the glass-fronted cage of the studio,
poor Mr Allen mouthed at me soundlessly through the
glass partition: I couldn't hear a word. Desperately I
twisted every knob, turned every switch on the control-
board—but to no avail. The eminent critic's lips continued to move, like a film-actor's when the sound-track
has broken down; I continued, vainly, to shout at him
through the glass; but we might, for all the sound that
emerged, have been yelling at one another across the
Grand Canyon. At last, humiliatingly, I was obliged to
rehearse the speaker in the studio itself, sitting at the
same table, and feeling extremely foolish. Mr Allen, a
kindly and tolerant soul, made no comment, though as
a practised broadcaster he must have found the pro-
cedure distinctly odd; mercifully for both of us, the
programme-engineer arrived just in time for the
transmission.

The Army had seemed to me very much like going back to school; and so, too, did the BBC, though the school, in this case, was of the most humane, progressive type, a kind of grown-up Bedales. In the Army one's mental age was assumed to be that of a rather backward prep-schoolboy, and one was treated accordingly; here, on the contrary, one was flatteringly assumed to be almost grown-up. From the start one was, so to speak, on back-slapping terms with the masters; a jolly Beda-lian spirit prevailed of work-of-each-for-weal-of-all, and any infringement of the rules would be interpreted, one felt, as a slur upon the Honour of the School. As a Talks Producer I felt myself to be a kind of glorified house-prefect, and I was uncomfortably aware, as I had been at school, of being temperamentally unfitted for so responsible a post.

As at Bedales, too, one was aware of being the in-heritor of a wholly modern, almost a revolutionary tradition: middle-aged survivors from the Savoy Hill period would recall the crude beginnings of broadcasting in much the same spirit of *laudator temporis acti* as visit-ing Old Bedalians used to boast of the pioneer days of co-education. There was indeed a vaguely co-educational quality about the BBC itself, a breezy atmosphere of sexual equality and sane-wholesome-comradeship which, for me, recalled vividly the prefects' common-room at Bedales.

I looked round my office: at the filing cabinet, the typewriters, the telephones—symbols of an alien, grown-up world to which I felt that I didn't really be-

long. Below the windows Langham Place lay sub-
merged beneath a thin greenish fog which, seeping into
the stuffy room, caught at the throat like a whiff of
chlorine. Across the road I could just distinguish the
gutted shell of the Queen's Hall—for this London to
which I had come, and in which, despite long familiarity,
I still felt a stranger, was the drab, peeling, melancholy
London of the post-war period; rationing was still in
force, social life retained much of its war-time austerity,
at the parties I went to there seemed a uniform and depressing lack of gaiety. I had been at the BBC nearly
three months: for the first time in my life, I was leading
an active and varied social life; in a rather dim way, I felt
myself to be 'in the swim'. In the way of business, I had
met a number of distinguished fellow-writers, some of
whom had become my friends; but the profession of
authorship had lost much of its glamour for me, I no
longer derived the *frisson* from meeting celebrities
which, in my youth, had occasionally rewarded my
sorties into Fitzrovia. I felt depressed, dissatisfied and
rather ill.

Much of my time was necessarily spent in trotting to
and fro between the Langham and Broadcasting House;
my office was overheated, so were the studios, and since
the weather was unusually bleak, I had begun to suffer
from perpetual colds and sore-throats. I had, moreover,
fallen a too-easy victim to another and more insidious
occupational disease of broadcasting: the chronic hang-
over. The strain imposed by an ever-widening circle of
acquaintance could only be mitigated by alcohol, and I
found myself caught up, inevitably, in the vicious circle

of hangovers and hairs-of-the-dog. For one like myself, by temperament a solitary, such an existence is apt to set up a sense of guilt which, paradoxically, can only be assuaged by a progressive increase in social activity; after a time I began positively to dread the prospect of eating a meal by myself, and, failing all else, would ring up old friends whom I hadn't seen for years and invite them (greatly to their astonishment) to lunch or dine with me.

It would be untrue—and unfair to the BBC—to say that I was unhappy; I enjoyed my work and liked most of my colleagues; but I realized, by now, that I was a fish out of water. I was possessed, as always, by the recurrent itch to write, and I knew that, if I continued in my present way of life, I should never put pen to paper again. I suffered, in consequence, from a perpetual, nagging sense of frustration; even the Army—though it had kept me busy enough—seemed, in retrospect, a less stringent form of captivity. I didn't, I think, even at the time, blame the BBC for my growing discontent; the fault, I realized, was entirely mine; and the BBC had at least one advantage over the Army—one could leave it at a month's notice. . . .

The sensation of Leaving Under a Cloud is one with which, during a mis-spent life, I have become all too familiar, and my departure from the BBC followed what for me has become a well-worn pattern. I was haunted by an uneasy feeling that, by leaving at such short notice, I was Letting Down the Side—which indeed I was. By now I had been allotted spaces for at least six months

ahead, and had contracted quite a number of speakers;
these would have to be handed over to other producers,
who wouldn't thank me for adding to their burdens.
Plainly I wasn't going to be very popular.

'I can't think what Mr Boyd will say, or Miss
Somerville either,' my secretary commented dis-
couragingly.

'Nor can I,' I echoed—untruthfully, as it happened,
for I knew only too well what Mr Boyd would say, and
Miss Somerville too. More than ever did I feel like a
member of the eleven who has inconsiderately gone
down with measles just before the Big Match. My de-
fection, I felt, would be construed as an act of disloyalty
towards the Headmaster: I half-expected to be summoned to the office of the Director-General, Sir
William Haley, for a 'little talk'. . . . Apart, however,
from a rather sticky interview with the Administrative
Officer of the Talks Department, who appealed (though
unsuccessfully) to my better nature, I was spared any
such valedictory homilies. The last few days were spent
in handing over my various commitments to other producers; everybody was very kind and helpful, and my
sense of guilt was in consequence redoubled. The last
day came, and I walked out of the Langham into the
chilly April dusk: my career as a Talks Producer had
lasted exactly four months.

I had come to London—in the professional sense—
late in life, my sojourn there had been brief and inglori-
ous, and I was thankful enough to be leaving it again.
One can't, of course, generalize from one's own case:
for some writers the urban ambience may provide just

the kind of stimulus they need; for others—and I suspect they are in a majority—life in London tends progressively to inhibit the creative faculty, and is liable, unless one is more than usually tough, to prove finally stultifying.

Rose Macaulay

WHEN I first used to come to London it was from our home in Italy, whence two parents and about five children travelled over to England every now and then to visit our relations. We would arrive in London carrying string bags and satchels bulging with those of our smaller personal possessions that could not be left behind, such as pocket knives, water pistols, books, paintboxes, mouth organs, and so on. We would all stay for a time with our grandmother in Gordon Place, Kensington. She would say to us each morning, 'Now children go and play in the streets while mother and I talk.' So we went out to play in the streets, while our grandmother and our mother talked, and our father read books in the British Museum and hunted about it for lost manuscripts which he hoped he would find, as he did in the libraries in Florence and Rome, and this was a whole-time occupation, so he could not take us about London much.

On the first morning in London we went to a shop called Theobald. I think this was somewhere in Clerkenwell Road but it is long since gone; we always wrote letters to it from Italy, ordering things to be sent us from its catalogue, so that to see it in the flesh was very romantic and exciting. We spent most of the money we

had there, and this money came from our uncles' tips,
our uncles being very kind and noble-hearted men. So
we bought from Theobald ships, magnets, pistols,
cannons, knives and other tools, roller-skates, mercury,
lead for melting, and many other very useful things, so
that after shopping there we had plenty to amuse ourselves with in the streets round our grandmother's
house. It was a good neighbourhood, because there was
a narrow passage running down by St Mary Abbott's
Church, where we could roller-skate and skip and spin
tops and walk on stilts and play hide and seek in and
around the church and churchyard. This passage is still
there, but much changed and less romantic; it used to
smell of vaseline. Then we would go into the High
Street and go up and down in Derry and Tom's lifts, up
in one and down in another, till the lift attendants grew
tired of us, which before long they did. After that we
would go into High Street Kensington station and buy
1½d tickets to the next station, and get into the sooty
train and travel all round the Inner Circle, which took
about an hour, and when we got out at High Street
again we were black with soot and choking, like chim-
ney sweeps, but we felt we had had a fine lot of travelling for three halfpence and had swindled the Railway
Company. So then we took our boats to the Round
Pond and sailed them. One day we went to Baker Street,
and looked for number 221A because of Holmes and
Watson, but we could not find it, so we walked along
Baker Street tracking criminals and noting where they
went, and more than once we thought we saw Watson,
who was more frequent then than now, but we never

saw Holmes with his deerstalker and ulster and cocaine,
searching the pavement for clues.

Sometimes a parent or uncle would take us to the
Zoo, or the Tower, or the Natural History Museum.
But mostly we played alone and did as we liked, and
looking back I see that on the whole we behaved in a
most uncultured way, for we did not really know at all
how people behaved in London, particularly on Sunday,
when, except for us, the streets round about Gordon
Place were very quiet. We had been brought up to use
Sunday as a day for unrestricted license and liberty and
riotous living, on account of having no lessons on that
day, and this came partly from living in Italy but more
from the excellent notions our parents had, and our
grandmother had had before. No one seemed to mind
our behaving like street arabs in London, and we
thought London was fine, and we had a very good time
there. We went to Earls Court and Olympia and rode on
scenic railways and down water-shoots and saw the
tournament and a few plays, and enjoyed it all enorm-
ously.

Having left Italy and settled in university towns, first
Oxford then Cambridge, my father went on reading in
libraries and hunting for and finding lost manuscripts in
the Bodleian and the Cambridge library, and my mother
was not strong, so we no longer came up to London as a
family. But, after I took up with writing, I began to
come up by myself. Rupert Brooke, who was an old
friend of ours, was often there after he had gone down
from King's, staying with Eddie Marsh; he wrote to me
from Gray's Inn, 'He is a delightful person to stay with,

he is so much away.' I sometimes went up to meet
Rupert for lunch or dinner and plays, and his friends,
who were apt to be poets, such as Edward Thomas and
Wilfred Gibson and Ralph Hodgson and others, sometimes came to lunch too, usually at the Moulin d'Or. I
was envious of Rupert, who walked about the streets
without a map, often with a plaid rug over his shoulders,
as if he was Tennyson, which seemed to me a very good
idea and gave him prestige, and people turned to look
at him as he strolled through Soho with his golden hair
and his rug, and I was proud to be with him. Rupert and
I used to go in for the *Saturday Westminster* Problems,
which were usually writing poems, and we both won
quite a lot of prizes for this. This Problems page was
edited by Naomi Royde-Smith, and we both wanted to
meet her; Rupert had heard that she was 'frightfully
amusing'. I forget which of us met her first, but I met
her sometime between 1910 and 1912, and was dazzled,
for she was amusing and interesting and brilliant, and
had beauty, and almost more charm than anyone else.
She was very kind to me. Through her I met her friend
Walter de la Mare. (I never, by the way, heard him
called Walter, but always either W.J. or Jack.) He was
very beautiful, and had a fantastic wit and funniness, and
his poetry was exquisite and full of ghosts and shadows
and dreams, as well as sometimes of a charming nonsense that seemed to belong to some strange moonish
world, and was different in kind from all other nonsense.
In his serious as well as his nonsense poetry he wholly
blurred the frontiers of reality and dream, which is what
poetry ought to do, for we do not want to know which is

which, but to travel about freely in both countries, not
hampered either by facts or dreams. His mind and the
cadences of his verse had a delicate, reticent wildness
that no other poet has exactly had.

Apart from his poetry, he was a fascinating and
fantasy-chasing conversationalist, and I fell deeply in
love both with him and with Naomi Royde-Smith. He
and she with her gay and ridiculous wit and her wide
literary range and critical appreciation, fitted exactly together. She too had a delightful appearance, and was one
of the rare exceptions to the general rule that men are
the better talkers. Another exception was her friend
Mary Agnes Hamilton, a brilliantly gifted intellectual,
then writing novels, later to be a Labour M.P., a dele-
gate to the League of Nations, a Governor of the BBC,
and a lot of fine things like that.

Naomi Royde-Smith was the centre of a lively and
able circle of friends. Like Mrs Montague, the queen of
of the blues, she did not encourage idiots. With her I
met, in this pre-war golden age, a number of people who
seemed to me, an innocent from the Cam, to be more
sparklingly alive than any in my home world. Some were
journalists, and worked on the literary side of the
Westminster; these seemed to know everything that was
behind the news; some, like J. R. Brooke, were civil
servants, and seemed to know even more that was behind the news, and the contemporary literary, political
and social scene became, to my inexperienced eyes, very
amusing and alive. Altogether, these people seemed to
me to be the people I felt at home with and liked to
know, and I wished that I too lived in London, with

whose inhabitants I had fallen collectively in love.

At that time, though I met a number of interesting people, mostly writers, I naturally did not, coming up occasionally as I did, meet most of the people I was later to know, and I cannot now remember when I met whom. I did not keep a diary, as so many writers seem to have always done; at least, my diary was entirely (as it is still) in the future tense, 'dine with so and so', not 'dined'. Some writers must have put down in their diaries not merely that they lunched or dined with so and so, but whom they met there, and what they all said. I sometimes thought it would be interesting to do this, so that in the evening of my life I could sit by the fire and read about myself when young; but it would have taken too much time and trouble, so here I am in the evening of my life with nothing of that kind to read, but actually I should not have time to sit and read it if I had, also it would have been bombed in 1941, when all my letters went, and all those little engagement diaries in the future tense. So I am uncertain about dates. I do not know which year it was that I dined with J. R. Brooke in the Temple and met his friends E.V. and R. A. Knox. I think R. A. Knox had not yet joined the Unreformed Church, but was still writing witty Anglican books; he and E. V. were both brilliant talkers, and the Knox wit scintillated like fireworks through the evening. At Naomi Royde-Smith's evening parties in Chelsea, or lunching with her in Fleet Street (in those days we lunched in small inexpensive restaurants, the standard of living and entertaining among writers being much less de luxe than it has since become) I met Hugh

Walpole, rosy with success and very cheerful and pleasant and friendly. He had his dog Jacob on a lead and
talked mostly about novels and novelists, for he took
this topic very seriously and sometimes even gave
lectures on it. A good deal seemed to be written about
it, then as now, for, like poetry, it is an apparently in-
exhaustible theme. I do not exactly remember who were
being most talked about just before 1914, but I know
there were a great many of them. In those days more
than now there was, I think, a kind of hierarchy of
Olympians, older and more important than the others,
such as Henry James, Hardy Shaw, Wells, Conrad, Max
Beerbohm, Yeats, Bridges, and perhaps a little lower
down the slope Belloc, Masefield, Chesterton, May
Sinclair, Somerset Maugham, and Elizabeth Russell,
who, with Max and Saki, was among the wittiest and
most verbally dexterous novelists then writing. Younger
than these there was a host of writers in the twenties
and thirties; some were good, some less good, some are
famous today, others almost forgotten, for oblivion
blindly scattereth her poppies, and some are quite
covered up by them and some not, and it seems largely
chance.

I suppose the most distinguished of the younger
novelists before 1914 was E. M. Forster; in 1913 he
was under 35, but had written all his novels but *A
Passage to India*, and held a position among writers
which was like no one else's. I did not meet him until I
came to live in London, in the 1920s. Virginia Woolf
had not yet started. D. H. Lawrence had published, I
think, two books. James Joyce had written *Portrait of an*

C.T.L.—L

Artist, and he and Dorothy Richardson (but she had come first) had begun the 'stream of consciousness' novel which became presently so much the vogue. Dorothy Richardson's 'Miriam' novels were entirely original, and she should be more remembered as a pioneer. They were a little tiring, but they had the fascination of novelty; she had us plodding along a new trail. She was a minority writer; I do not think her reputation was ever wide, like that of Compton Mackenzie, who flashed through the pre-war years like a meteor, or even J. D. Beresford, who, more heavy-handedly, produced the Jacob Stahl trilogy and that *tour de force, The Hampdenshire Wonder.*

But there were scores of novelists, male and female, who seemed to themselves and their friends fairly eminent, and a lot of poets who seemed eminent too, and who read their poetry aloud in Harold and Alida Munro's Poetry Bookshop in Devonshire Street off Theobald's Road. I would often when in London go and hear this. I liked meeting the poets, who did not, however, read poetry very well, for few do this, and I would always rather read it to myself. The poetry of those days, being so much more sensuous and cadenced than it is today, and much less packed with meaning and symbols and intricate word arrangements, was easier to read well, but all the same it was seldom read well. De la Mare read his poetry deplorably, Yeats had his own incantatory manner, fascinating, peculiar, and eventually soporific. I forget if I heard Jack Squire, Ralph Hodgson, Lascelles Abercrombie, Edward Thomas, Martin Armstrong, or John Drinkwater reading at the

Bookshop, then or later. But there was a general interest in poetry in those days, far more than there is now. There seemed a kind of poetry-intoxication going about; this seems to have died out under the sobering influence of two wars and of a rather different fashion of verse, and now few people seem much interested in contemporary verse except those who write it. The Georgian Poets (which began to be published in 1912 under the editorship of Eddie Marsh) sold like novels; so, I think, did *New Numbers,* a series in which Rupert Brooke, Wilfred Gibson, John Drinkwater, and (I think) Lascelles Abercrombie got together to publish their verses. And from the Poetry Bookshop poured out broadsheets, ballads and chapbooks with coloured prints, very gay and engaging and naive, and suggestive of Roger Fry's Omega workshop.

There was also a great blossoming of literary magazines, which opened for a season and died. There was Ford Madox Hueffer's *English Review,* which published stories by E. M. Forster; Middleton Murry's and Katherine Mansfield's *Blue Review* (which published D. H. Lawrence) and *Rhythm;* and, more detonating and flashy, Wyndham Lewis's *Blast,* which ran futurism and vorticists and Marinetti. Marinetti was the vogue just then; his vehemence when he lectured was alarming.

It was, I suppose, a time of literary ferment. But more exciting than literature, because newer, was the Russian ballet, about which we all went mad in those years. It really was something to go mad about: it opened a new and enchanted world; those who missed it through being too young, or even, many of them, not born for some time after, missed something which they will never now see, for later ballet was not the same as those pre-war confections of Diaghileff and Massine and Nijinski and Pavlova and Lopokova and Karsavina, which only the old and middle-aged can now remember. I saw the *Sylphides*, the *Lac des Cygnes*, the *Spectre de la Rose*, *Thamar*, *L'Après Midi d'un Faune*, and, I think, the *Sacre du Printemps*. Meanwhile Caruso and Melba were singing at Covent Garden, and Beecham had his Russian Opera season at Drury Lane, with Chaliapine in *Boris Godunof*, *Prince Igor*, and *Ivan the Terrible*. London blazed with stars; looking back from our drabber age, one sees it through a romantic haze, which spread over everything. The Vedrenne Barker Company were producing Shaw at the Court; I came up to see *Fanny's First Play* and *Pygmalion*. Masefield's *Nan*, *The Wild Duck*, and Granville Barker's Shakespeare at the Savoy, brilliant in colour and texture.

It became easier to see plays, because before the end of 1913 my uncle gave me a flat; it was in a Safe Deposit in Southampton Buildings off Chancery Lane, and for the first time in my life I had a home of my own, where I used to spend part of each week. I had a small housewarming party there; I forget exactly who came, but certainly W. J. de la Mare did, and Naomi Royde-Smith, and Frank Sidgwick, and Rupert, and Iolo Williams, and some other poets. It wasn't an ambitious party, there wasn't much to eat or drink, so far as I remember, but we played paper games and it was great fun at the time, and part of the sociable London life which seemed so happy, clever, exciting and good.

What puzzles me as I look back is the contrast between social life as we led it (whether in London or
Cambridge) and the way it struck some others who
remember it. I was reading lately Sir Lawrence Jones's
An Edwardian Youth, which was, of course, Edwardian
not Georgian, but his account of society, and particularly of how there was no way of getting to know
women and girls well, because young men and women
did nothing together, except dancing, struck me as most
strange, and quite different from any social life I knew.
Of course he moved in more upper-class and conven-
tional circles than I and my friends, and writers are
notoriously free in their habits, but it still seems odd
that there should have been all that difference. Because
in my world young men and women shared work and
amusements, played games together, went out together
in the evenings, went country walking together (we did
not call it hiking, but we did more of it), discussed
everything together, and, in fact, behaved much as they
do now, except that there was much less going to bed
together.

Anyhow, life was gay and amusing and civilized.
Behind all the talking and the writing and the ballet and
the theatres and the poetry, there were a few quite uncivilized noises off, from Ireland, and from the Balkans,
and from strikers and suffragettes. Not being politically
minded, I do not think that I attended very closely.
Naturally I knew it was ridiculous to deprive half the
people of the country of any voice in the laws they had
to live under, merely on account of trifling difference in

sex; but I did not feel that anything I could do about it was likely to be helpful.

Then came the loudest and most uncivilized of the noises off, a chapter was closed with a bang, and the world ran amok like a herd of wild elephants.

That golden age will not return: and anyhow one has grown too old for it.

COMING TO LONDON : 14
Edith Sitwell

I HAD, from my earliest childhood, spent part of each year in London; but it was not until the second year of World War I that I arrived there as a Ticket of Leave Woman—in partial freedom from the lifelong imprisonment to which my parents had hoped to condemn me.

I then knew nobody in the world of the arts excepting Walter Sickert, who had always, since I was 17 and met him for the first time, shown me great kindness, and my enchanting cousin by marriage, Mrs George Swinton, the singer, in whose house I met him.

Elsie Swinton turned all days to glamour; in her presence, the thoughts of rain or of dullness could not exist; all the lights and colours and excitement of summer came and went in one's head.

But it was not until much later that I made frequent excursions into 'intellectual society'—this being difficult for me, because my entire lack of culture of any kind was perceived immediately. I was not original in my conduct —on the other hand, my poetry was regarded as revolutionary: (whereas, to be popular, my *conduct* should have been revolutionary, and my *poetry* should not). My furniture was not made of tin, ostrich feathers did not trail on my floor, I had never hit anybody with a bottle, and avoided those circles in which this was regarded as a sign of mental superiority.

167

'Intellectual society' was, at that time, divided into two camps, and to neither of these did I, by nature, belong. On the one side was the school of thought to which I have just referred, and to which I could not, by nature of my sex, upbringing, tastes, and lack of muscle, belong. On the other side was the society of Bloomsbury, the home of an echoing silence. This society was described to me by Gertrude Stein as 'The Young Men's Christian Association—with Christ left out, of course.'

Here are a few butterfly aspects of the life I saw at that time—butterfly aspects only.

A major Bloomsbury royalty at that time was Lytton Strachey; I knew him but slightly. He made the impression on me of the benevolent demons in the Russian ballet *Children's Tales*—a demon with a long beard of gardener's bass, and a head which existed only in profile. He seemed to have been cut out of rather thin cardboard. He wasted no words. A young and robustious friend of ours, meeting him at a party, said 'you don't remember me, Mr Strachey. We met four years ago.' 'Quite a nice interval, I think, don't you?' Mr Strachey remarked, pleasantly, and passed on.

Remembering to forget, or, as the Marx brothers put it, 'buying back introductions' was a great feature at the time. It was said—I do not know with what truth—that a certain very great sculptor, on finding the late Mark Gertler at the Café Royal, said to him 'Gertler, do you remember the time when we were not acquainted?' Gertler said that he had some dim recollection of it. 'Let us go back to that time, Gertler!' said the great man.

I knew Roger Fry well, for I sat to him for several portraits. For one of these, I wore a lily-green evening gown, and my appearance in this, in the full glare of midday, and in Fitzroy Square, together with the appearance of Mr Fry, his bushy, rather long grey hair floating from under an enormous black hat, caused great joy to the children of the district, as we crossed from Mr Fry's studio to his house for luncheon. Imagining us to be strayed revellers, they inquired at moments (perhaps not unnaturally) if our mothers knew we were out. At other moments they referred to a certain date in November when, according to them, our appearance would have been better timed.

Mr Fry was a singularly delightful companion, learned and courteous, and had a great gift for attracting and retaining friendship. Warm-hearted, generous-minded, chivalrous, and kindly, he was always espousing some lost cause, championing some unfortunate person, rushing at some windmill with a lance. In other respects he was dreamy and vague, and incapable of noticing any but a spiritual discomfort. I remember an incident when I was having luncheon in his house after a sitting. Mr Fry's slippers could not be found anywhere, and a game of hunt-the-slipper ensued. But in the middle of the fun, a loud crash was heard, and a hoarse voice said 'Coal, Sir.' 'Put it, my good man,' said Mr Fry, whirling round and round like a kitten chasing its tail, losing his spectacles, and speaking in a vague voice weak with fatigue—'Oh, well, put it on the bed.' At this point, I found the slippers in a milk-jug, and the fun stopped.

People who knew Mr Fry well spent much of their time in inventing affectionate legends about him, and these, though having usually no foundation in actual fact, often bore a strong spiritual resemblance to him.

There was, for instance, the legend about his painting wallpaper for his house at Guildford. It was rumoured that, having placed long strips of the uncoloured paper on his studio floor (rather as if the strips were railway lines) he would gallop along them on hands and knees at a terrific speed, armed with a paintbrush. From time to time, hypnotized by this onrush, a cup of coffee would, of its own volition, hurl itself on to it, or Mr Fry's faithful dog would seat himself, firmly, upon the wet paint, leaving a deep indentation. But Mr Fry was in no way disturbed or put out: 'Really, *Rath-er* and *interesting* result,' he would mumble, as he rushed along at a hundred miles an hour.

This story, though characteristic, is probably—I can only say probably—untrue. So may be the story that Mr Fry invented an instrument, consisting of a piece of string and a lump of lead, that would register the exact amount of emotion felt by the person holding it, when brought, for the first time, into the presence of a great work of art. The legend goes that Mr Fry was taken, for the first time (string in hand) into the presence of a green apple painted by Cézanne, and that the apparatus went completely beserk, striking him violently, first in the stomach, and then upon the forehead, and knocking him unconscious.

One of our greatest friends at that time, as he is now, was Arthur Waley. In all these years he has not changed, his singularly beautiful, ascetic face having remained the same as it was when we knew him first.

Our stories about him are endless—and many of them are true.

Dr Waley is very gentle and unassuming, though anyone looking at him would realize they were seeing a man of great intellectual attainments.

His courteous silence, whilst laying him open to being victimized by bores, always makes him victorious in the end. On one occasion, a young man who was a phenomenon of dullness was brought to my flat, and seeing Dr Waley sitting there so quietly (he was entirely ignorant of Dr Waley's identity) was inspired to floods of eloquence. 'As a humble but accredited member of His Majesty's Diplomatic Service, Sir' boomed the young man, 'about to be sent to Japan, can you by any chance, tell me what is the attitude of the People of the Chrysanthemum towards the King Emperor?' 'None,' replied Dr Waley on an upward note, and stared in front of him. 'And what, Sir, is the attitude of the People of the Rising Sun towards Woman?' 'None' (the note still higher and fainter). At this point, my attention was distracted by Dr Waley's nervous fellow guests, but the young man's voice boomed on and on. 'And I presume, Sir, that I shall meet you at one time or another in Japan?' 'No.'— 'But you have evidently a great knowledge of Japanese literature and life?' 'Yes.'

The young gentleman then became silent, though not with such an impenetrable silence as that of Dr Waley, whose Chinese impassivity seemed to grow deeper. I do not know if the young gentleman ever discovered to whom he had been talking.

My great time for party-going was from 1918 to the middle-thirties. Everything then seemed bathed in glamour: it was always summer.

Most of the parties were fun; but some were not.

There were the parties of Lady X, the wife of an Emperor of Finance. These always held unexpected possibilities.

Lady X was separated from the Emperor, but was expected to uphold his position. From time to time, a message would reach her, borne by one of the discreet nation of secretaries to be found in the Emperor's house —(confidential secretaries, business secretaries, financial secretaries, social secretaries) conveying Lord X's disapproval. Lady X was not spending enough money. More must be spent immediately. It was due to his position.

In a panic, Lady X would buy fifty gold cigarette cases, and would shower these on the more impecunious of the young men of her acquaintance.

Then came the word, 'The Arts must be patronized!' This threw her into an even greater panic. How was she to patronize the arts when she did not know which one, or even the name of one of the practitioners.

Then she remembered. An old Belgian lady had told her she had a nephew who was a poet. The very thing! The poet was imported. He was a terrible, very young man in a tulip-mauve suit, and had large, liquid, over-expressive dark eyes. His verses were even more dreadful than he was. But they were very fashionable. This

was in the early 'twenties, and to be in the fashion they
had to be printed in alternating lines of green, black,
violet, and red. Sometimes the lines would read downwards (as in Chinese literature) sometimes they would
slant, from high on the right-hand corner to low on the
left, or, again, from low on the left to high on the right,
but only very occasionally would they be printed plain,
like yours and mine.

Lady X saw, very clearly, that he was exactly what
she was looking for. At enormous expense, she had the
poems printed in a limited edition of 5,000 on hand-
made paper. But Lord X, by some sixth sense (for he
had not seen the poems) divined that they were so
terrible they must never be allowed to see the light of
day. So Lord X requested one of his secretaries (usually
a confidential one) to repair at crack of dawn on the day
when the edition was to be sent for review, and to buy
up the whole edition. This he would do, at the same
time hinting to the publishers the fate that would inevitably overtake them if they did not fall in with the
Business Emperor's wishes.

Lady X could not understand what had happened.
Why were there no reviews? And *why* should the whole
edition have been snapped up almost before the publisher's office opened? She ordered, quickly, a second
edition. The same thing happened. It was a mystery!
The third edition. The same!

After that, the history eludes me. But I think Lord X
must have come to the conclusion that Lady X had better
give the Arts a miss, and give parties instead.

She did, and these were many (she was an extremely

kind and hospitable woman). But the parties were a
source of some terror to the younger among her guests,
because their elders seemed always to be in a state of
guerrilla warfare.

At that time, I was a near neighbour of Aldous and
Maria Huxley, and, when my brothers were away, we
nearly always went to parties together. 'Dear me!' I
remember Aldous saying, sinking wearily into a chair,
just after we had received another invitation from Lady
X. 'What can we say *now?* Let me consider, please!
How about "Mr and Mrs Aldous Huxley and Miss
Edith Sitwell thank Lady X for her last thirty-two invitations, which they regret they are unable to accept as
all three are suffering from contagious epilepsy".'

A party to which I look back with great pleasure was
one given by a certain art critic, now dead. He gave it in
order to help a rather ageing gentleman who had found
himself in the plight of acting as publicity agent to a
former artists' model who had decided, late in life, to
adopt the career of dancer. (It is unknown for what
reason.)

In a spirit of duty, Mr Z, the agent in question, had
declared in a Sunday newspaper that, Maharajahs were
in the habit of pouring rubies into the lap of this lady in
restaurants, and that hostesses were falling over each
other to secure her services for their parties. But as my
brother Sacheverell said to me sadly, the only hostess
who was really falling over himself was the art critic in
question.

On the afternoon of the party, we were met on the
steps of our host's house by the dancer, Mr Z, and

eleven young men with blond hair and long eyelashes who had been recruited from the chorus of a musical comedy, and instructed to rush after the dancer like moths to a candle, to bend over her, and to exhibit signs of an almost insane infatuation and delight. Mr Z was afraid (not without reason) that they might forget their instructions, so he told the drummer of the band to keep an eye on them, and, if they flagged for an instant, to beat a furious tattoo.

All went fairly well until the dancer took the floor. To watch her then, was like watching a four-wheeler, heavily laden, leaving a station.

An old gentleman, sitting next to me, inquired in a loud voice, 'What is she doing *that* for?'

Alas, like so many of Mr Z's schemes, this eventually faded out. But trying to be of use to Mr Z was, at that time, in the nature of a national industry.

It is sad to think that our acquaintance ended as it did.

Mr Z was, unfortunately, suddenly seized by an inspiration, and, a prey to this, composed a drama which —so he assured my brother Osbert—was in blank verse, and which recorded the sufferings of those ill-starred lovers Paolo and Francesca.

This he insisted on Osbert reading. (We had not, at that time, developed our present virtuosity in dealing with senders of manuscripts.)

It was thought by my family that Dante had already chronicled these sufferings adequately, and that there the matter might have been left. But no. Mr Z was adamant.

My brother sighed, put down the MS and went for

a walk. When he returned, the treasure, which was the size of the week's laundry in a station hotel, had vanished.

It was not until very many months afterwards, on one of the infrequent occasions when both the cat and her offspring were absent from her basket at the same time, that it was discovered that the work had been used to line this. Unfortunately, when found, the work bore not only but too evident traces that it had been subjected to the inevitable *va-et-vient* and general wear and tear attendant on the cat's frequent accouchements and nursing operations, but it looked, also, as if it had been torn by tigers!

My brother wished to have the manuscript re-typed —but not a line of it was decipherable, and, had it not been for Dante, the fate of the ill-starred lovers would have remained for ever a mystery.

Then came the problem—how to tell Mr Z the fate that had befallen his masterpiece, and the *reason!* The mind boggles, faced with such a situation!

Nature has supervened on our behalf, wrapping us in a blissful forgetfulness of the outcome of the matter.

All we remember is, that from then onwards, our lives and the life of Mr Z ran in different channels.